Bringing Our Souls to the Classroom

Rob D'Alessio

BALBOA PRESS
A DIVISION OF HAY HOUSE

Balboa Press books may be ordered through booksellers or by contacting:

Balboa Press
A Division of Hay House
1663 Liberty Drive
Bloomington, IN 47403
www.balboapress.com
1-(877) 407-4847

ISBN: 978-1-4525-3262-2 (sc)
ISBN: 978-1-4525-3264-6 (hc)
ISBN: 978-1-4525-3263-9 (e)

Library of Congress Control Number: 2011902113

Printed in the United States of America

Balboa Press rev. date: 3/1/2011

"Stop acting as if life is a rehearsal. Live this day as if it were your last. The past is over and gone. The future is not guaranteed."

- Dr. Wayne Dyer

CONTENTS

INTRODUCTION

I make a positive difference in my students' lives.
-teacher affirmation-

Eighty percent of first graders have high self-esteem. Just five percent of ninth graders do! These ninth graders have less determination, less hope, and less faith. We as teachers have the power to change this thereby making our jobs easier. And if we change the attitude of students in our class we actually change the school, because our students will rub off on other students. We know this because we know that our thoughts and feelings affect other people's mind and/or body. How often have you been in a bad mood and quickly affected the mood of those around you as a result? And I believe that the closer you are to the person/people, the greater the effect. Think back to when you were a child of five or six and your mother or father was very upset or very sad... your mood instantly changed to correspond.

I would be in my tenth year of teaching before I finally made the affirmation: "I speak positively with others and listen with compassion." That is to say, for the first time in my life and career, I had a genuine desire to speak positively and listen with compassion much to the delight of my higher-self and much to the dismay of my 'pain body.' If you have ever read Echart Tolle, you know what 'pain body' means but if you have not, just know that it refers to that part of our ego which feeds off negativity or as Dexter would call it, "the dark passenger." I also spent over nine years envying those co-workers who came across to me as so positive, optimistic, and lucky. Not only that but I knew that to them, I must have come across as impatient, incapable of handling stress, and generally unlucky. Eventually, I realized that everything happens in its own time for your best and highest good. And I trust that this is so. Consider the following quote by Charles R. Swindoll: "The longer I live, the more I realize the impact of attitude on life. Attitude, to me, is more important than facts. It is more important than the past, the education, the money, than circumstances, than failure, than successes, than what other people think or say or do. It is more important than appearance, giftedness or skill. It will make or break a company... a church... a home. The remarkable thing is we have a choice everyday regarding the attitude we will embrace for that day. We cannot change our past... we cannot change the fact that people will act in a certain way. We cannot change the inevitable. The only thing we can do is play on the one string we have, and that is our attitude. I am convinced that life is 10% what happens to me and 90% of how I react to it. And so it is with you... we are in charge of our attitudes." So if 90% of life has to do with how we react than, our subconscious minds are the driving force of our lives. Motivational speaker Alvin Law spoke at the 2010 Ontario Students Leadership Conference in Niagara Falls that I had the pleasure of chaperoning, and he was born with no arms and found success, joy, and the wife, children, and career he wanted. He said "you always hear people saying you need to think positively.... Well dah! Everybody knows that! It's all about attitude."

But is it that simple?

Is the single motivating power of our entire life, our feelings which are of the subconscious mind? If so, it's funny, I don't remember learning in Teachers' College that subconscious programs control ninety-five percent of our behavior. Moreover, I was never taught about affirmations, conventional clinical hypnotherapy, or energy psychology.

Did you know that our observations effect reality?

Did you know that when we are told something about ourselves or say something to ourselves about ourselves, for better or for worse, it is an affirmation that has an impact on us?

Do you agree that the purpose of life is joy?

Have you heard of stories of teachers transforming students with gratitude?

Are you grateful when you have a class you love or do you only notice when you have a class that you would rather not have and are you aware of the different effect this has on your life?

Are you happy to see your students enter the room or are you relieved when they are dismissed?

Author Louise Hay once had a teacher who told her she could never dance because she was too tall. My grade six teacher told my parents that I could never go to university. In both cases, we were guided by these negative affirmations that delayed or impeded our goals.

Being stuck in fear versus trusting the path before you is a complicated thing. But we need to make it simple so we can teach it. This book isn't just about praising students and teaching them that they can do anything they put their mind to, but it is also about using affirmations in the classroom to create the most peaceful classroom we can imagine. But to use affirmations in the classroom you must first use them at home. So we will talk a little about affirmations in general but I strongly feel that teachers need to read Louise Hay and/or Norman Vincent Peale, and/or Ester & Jerry Hicks to learn all about affirmations. You can also Google all sorts of creative affirmations that will help you become more of a clear thinker and thereby a more exemplary teacher.

"Ideas come to be effortlessly" is an example of an affirmation that anyone can use but a very good one for teachers. I knew a co-worker once that never used a day book. I can't imagine that. But there have been times where my day book was not only non- supply- teacher- friendly but not user-friendly to me and therefore not productive for my class. I use affirmations that specifically refer to my day book and make me more organized and I have just now begun to put actual daily affirmations right into the day book and lesson plans. Give it a try.

Before reading any further, however, be open to the fact that you need to learn how to love yourself through affirmations for any of the suggestions in this book to work. This means being content with yourself to come across as happy. This is so important. Our students know when we are happy and when we are stressed, indifferent, angry, or tired, this comes across loud and clear especially to what we call behavior problem students. I had a principal once who did not have children but had dogs; she was a dog-lover always making dog analogies for students. It was a bit much, but one thing was true, dogs behave adorably around us when they sense we are calm and happy and if they sense fear and stress they may harass us. So that principal's analogies sometimes were relevant and helpful.

There is a difference between goals and affirmations. Goals can often be thought of as things that may happen someday, somehow. An example of a goal and affirmation that are one in the same would be: "I take a moment to see myself in the perfect job. I visualize myself in that environment which is completely fulfilling--while I earn a good salary. I hold this vision for me and know that it has been fulfilled in consciousness..."

My favorite show of all time is *Lost*. The show was about an island mysterious by its magnetism. So it is with affirmations. They are mysterious. In our lifetime, we never will fully understand them. But by just realizing the fact that consciousness is made of energy, plus the fact that we already know that energy includes electricity and magnetism, we become open to infinite positive possibilities. It may be true that the practice of affirmations come more naturally to some than others but to think that this is unfair would be a negative affirmation. On *Lost*, Kate was living a life where one bad thing led to another but she was a good person (though some might argue she was not) who was one of the most positive people on the island. Her crashing on the island turned out to be the best thing that could have happened to her and her attitude acknowledged that. She was one of the people who survived and got off the island. On this mysterious island where money could have no meaning, would you assume that people would change their personalities accordingly? The lovable character, Hurley, wins a super lottery jackpot right before the plane crash. He had always considered himself to be unlucky and figured it was par to the course that he be on the plane that would crash right after the lottery winnings something that Alanis Morisssete would call "ironic". In an alternate sideways timeline which I interpreted as a Purgatory-matrix, the plane never crashes and Hurley goes on to invest his millions into billions but never changes who he is, he does not become corrupt or less lovable. So many of our students have the wrong idea about money don't they? They seem split between money is corrupt and therefore corrupts versus money is the key to success. Of course money is not the key to success. Some of us get carried away, however, and go around preaching that they would never want to win the lottery. There's a great book by Ori and Rom Brafman called *Sway* in which it clearly states and illustrates: "Managers, parents, and, of course, economists have long operated under the assumption that monetary incentives increase motivation. But psychologists are beginning to discover that the connection between the two is trickier than it first appears."

I want to share my ideas about affirmations in the life of a teacher with you. Love, joy, peace, and a sense of well being in our schools is the future and it has begun. We can change our classrooms for the better. Our thoughts are the tools towards this. This is what it is about as opposed to figuring out what incentives will work for our students. The logical incentive of wanting to do well in school so that one can get into college or university can be a waste of time. It is a meaningless incentive to a student who is affirming negative thoughts on a daily basis. In *Sway,* the authors go on to write: "Now, the problem isn't with rewards per se. It's only when you dangle the *possibility* of a reward ahead of time- creating a quid pro quo situation- that destructive effects arise..." We need to avoid making things worse in our classroom by trying things that make perfect sense to our functional-past brains but that don't have the capacity to work in the classroom effectively and consistently. Consider the following from *Sway,* " An extensive review and analysis of motivation studies found that the prospect of reward excites the pleasure center even more than the attainment of the reward itself. Taking a kid to Disneyland because she won the science fair is one thing, but telling her ahead of time, "If you enter the fair and win it, I'll take you to Disneyland," is another. It's that *anticipation* factor that drives the addictive behavior and suppresses the altruism center." Compensating star teachers whose students do well on standardized tests sounds all fine and well but the evidence is now overwhelming that it does not work. Merit-pay as supported by many politicians like President Obama, is as we now know, backwards-thinking. As it is concluded in *Sway,* "...throwing money into the mix diminishes altruistic motivation and introduces unexpected behavior." Conventional thinking in the education system will miss the mark. Dr. Wayne W. Dyer wrote in the foreword of Esther and Jerry Hicks's *Ask and It Is Given- Learning to manifest your Desires,* "When you change the way you look at things, the things you look at change." Maybe we need to change the way we view our students?

To understand this book you must know what is meant by "affirmations." An affirmation is anything you say or think. Positive patterns of affirmations bring about positive change. All we have to do is take responsibility. How many times have we talked about responsibility to or about our students? Every word and every thought we have create our classrooms. Our ability to create the best classroom is hindered by negative thoughts which are very tempting to have when we have stress in the classroom. But every time we get angry at a parent, student, policy, or the union or the board, we are affirming that we want more of it even though our conscious mind is repelled. Affirmations are simple yet complicated in that they won't work unless we do them right and sometimes that takes time. To quickly understand how to get them to work, consider what is written in Esther and Jerry Hicks's *Ask and It Is Given- Learning to manifest your Desires* about when an affirmation doesn't work, an example being: *"(Saying)* "I want this thing to happen that hasn't happened yet," not only activates the vibration of your desire, but you are also activating a vibration of the absence of your desire- so nothing changes for you." The first time I tried using affirmations I was left with regret. I felt like I had wasted time like when you get out of a long-term relationship that was crazy-dysfunctional. "But when you say, "Wouldn't it be nice if this desire would come to me?" you achieve a sort of expectation that is much less resistant in nature."

Negative affirmations win out because they are habitual. I spent a few years doing affirmations only once in a while and with less feeling then my negative affirmations and sometimes I would go several days without saying any affirmations. This led to the opposite of what I wanted happening. We need to understand that our students don't want to misbehave or fail an exam but they give off that impression when and if we do not consider the negative affirmations that are going on in their mind day in and day out.

Negative students and circumstances can change for the better or for the worse depending on our affirmations. I have been guilty of saying "I hate my job." This is one of the all time worst affirmations.

Louise Hay has stressed in several of her books and CDs that to counter the "I have a lousy job" affirmation, you can say this: "Wonderful new doors are opening for me all the time."

"All is well" is the default go-to affirmation to use not only in daily practice but in the classroom at the most stressful times, the results are miraculous.

But you may say "haven't we always told students to think positive?" It's simple, but it's not that simple. Dr. Bruce Lipton put it well in *Spontaneous Evolution- Our Positive Future*: " Perceptions shape the placebo... They are more influential than positive thinking because they are more than mere thoughts in your mind. Perceptions are beliefs that permeate every cell. Simply, the expression of the body is a compliment to the mind's perceptions, or, in simpler terms, *believing is seeing!*"

He and co-author Steve Bhaerman, go on to provide evidence that: "... the mind imagines who we think we are, but it controls only 5 percent or less of our lives. The data reveals what those of us who tried positive thinking but got negative results sadly came to realize that our lives are not controlled by our conscious wishes or intentions." You may say, "Well, aren't you contradicting yourself?" No, if we reverse that seventy percent of our thoughts are negative to seventy percent positive or sixty or even fifty percent, we will shape our subconscious. We can teach ourselves this and we can teach this to students in a variety of ways including modeling behavior, meditations, and journaling. I think it is important to be realistic and not try to imply that we can have 100% of our thoughts positive. Even Louise Hay admits that not all her thoughts are positive.

It is only now that teachers are beginning to realize that our words and actions are continuously recorded by our students' subconscious mind. So it's not just the parents who are affecting the students. Parents of behavior-problem- prone students are more often than not, quick to blame teachers. Parents blame teachers before they consider their own parenting as a culprit in their son/daughter's track record. Parents may have one more reason to blame us now if they have the knowledge that what we say and how we say it and what we think affects their children. Although, if they realize this, then some of them would realize that they are part of the reason their son or daughter misbehaves. Therein lies the ideal. We need the future generation to be mindful.

As teachers, we all know how frustrating it is when a student does something we deem deplorable and serious and then nothing happens in terms of consequences in the name of "mitigating circumstances". But as we will see, mindfulness provides a true understanding of mitigating reasons. A classic example, I say classic because it is an old common factor though we seldom consider it, is what a child we teach went through when they were in the womb for nine months before their birth. As Dr. Bruce Lipton and Steve Bhaerman illustrate: "When the mother thinks thoughts of rejection toward her fetus, the fetal nervous system programs itself with the emotion of rejection." You might think here, how on earth could a mother who opted not to have an abortion in the first place, could have feelings of not wanting her baby. But it happens all the time. A mother-to-be who has a very dysfunctional life and is very unhappy, believes that once she has a baby her life will be so much better via a new found source of happiness but the thought of raising the child, the finances and the responsibilities serve as an overpowering state of stress. And in fact I have personally known people in this situation and I want to say to them, "Stop the madness! Read Louise Hay!" But you can't change people. You can't change students. You can only change your own reality. Or if you can change students, this is not the right book, because it is about changing our own thinking patterns by using affirmations and mindfulness based pedagogy strategies and developing these strategies to model behavior in such a way that your class is a peaceful fun learning environment where positive energy can be harnessed. And though you may not change a dysfunctional student's overall attitude, they will be more likely to reach greater levels of success and be grateful to you for it, as Lipton and Bhaerman put it: "...whatever has been programmed can be deprogrammed and reprogrammed."

Practice the affirmations in this book and make your own. You will be so much better for it because you will have learned the important value of blessing, with love, your current job no matter how you feel about it (You drew it to you by your thinking. Bless your students, the building, parents, co-workers etc.). How can you expect good work from your students if they don't feel respected by you? Don't believe that it is hard to get a 'dream class.' Your consciousness will open the pathway to you. "Getting a dream class may be hard for some but not me" is a good job affirmation. You will know you serve others willingly and great things happen as a result.

CHAPTER I

AFFIRMATIONS

"The Universe always waits in smiling repose for us to align our thinking with its laws"

-Louise Hay-

Louise Hay once said and affirmed, "If I want to live in a peaceful world, then it is up to me to make sure that I am a peaceful person. No matter how others behave, I keep peace in my heart. I declare peace in the midst of chaos or madness. I surround all difficult situations with peace and love." Since she said and wrote that, millions of people have made the same affirmation and marveled at the positive changes in their lives.

One of the most beautiful affirmations that anyone can use comes from Louise Hay from *Inner Wisdom- Meditations for the Heart and Soul*:

> "When I begin to work on myself, sometimes things get worse before they get better. It is okay if that happens, because I know that it's the beginning of the process. It's untangling old threads. I just flow with it. It takes time and effort to learn what I need to learn. I don't demand

> instant change. Impatience is only resistance to learning. I let myself do it step by step..."

What are affirmations? On some level, we all know the answer. Many of you have seen the classic YouTube video where the cute little girl is in the mirror shouting out all the things in her life that she loves (http://www.your-inner-wisdom.com/index.htm). We know what a positive affirmation is and we know what positive thinking is but we tend to overlook and underestimate negative affirmations. It's very important that people not hate their jobs. We know this but we may not fully appreciate the amount of negative affirmations we recite when it comes to our jobs. The importance of actually loving one's job is of course especially true for teachers since hating our jobs effects our students and not just ourselves. There are four ways to tell if you need to like your job as a teacher more than you currently do: a) one way to tell if you do not like your job of course is if you genuinely dislike your principal, b) if you know in your heart of hearts that you are underperforming and not doing your best, c) you take twenty sick days a year yearly, and d) you know that students look forward to snow days but they aren't known to log on to the weather network's website to look at the five day forecast calculating the probability of a snow day, but somehow teachers tend to do just that, I know I used to (of course if your intention is purely because you know you will get a great deal of work done in the event of a snow day then it's less of a red flag); but anything that causes you to dread getting up in the morning and to always be counting down the days until the next snow day, PD Day, or holiday is concerning wouldn't you agree? So, do you hate your job?

I am writing this book after ten years in education. I'm by no means a veteran teacher yet but I am becoming an exemplary teacher. That it is something I could have been saying and affirming right from the get-go. Like most teachers, I have had good semesters and bad semesters and down right depressing semesters. In hindsight, it was at times when I thought I was cursed with the most unreasonable and unruly students and subsequently their equally unreasonable parents, that I myself was focusing on problems inside and outside of school. So naturally, they got worse. I say "naturally" but do you know why? It sounds right to say that but how is that natural? At my rock-bottom moments I made the rookie-mistake of focusing on my fears which naturally manifested (I can recall several summers where at the end of July, I would already start thinking about potential problem-students and parents that awaited me in September), and worse, I can recall many times looking at fellow teachers around me that I considered exemplary, and I in turn focusing on my limitations never moving beyond the thought that I was a good teacher or maybe just satisfactory.

In any event, if you are reading this you probably know what positive affirmations are. What you may not know, is how effective education-specific positive affirmations can be. With this book, I intend to promote professional development when it comes to mindfulness. Mindfulness in education is a wonderful solution to 98 percent of the problems in any education system. This involves combining professional development on mindfulness- based pedagogy, affirmations in the classroom, brain research, viewing the union as a professional association, differentiated instruction, coping with mitigating reasons, and becoming open to evolving compassion-based pedagogy. All this together will result in quickly infusing within your students a love of learning. This in turn will make teachers' jobs and lives a lot easier. As you read this, have a highlighter and highlight affirmations you wish to use. I also suggest buying a journal book or doing what I do, and use *The Secret Gratitude Book* by Rhonda Byrne (there are many other examples, Louise Hay has one too that works well, or use more than one). Write down things you want to begin affirming in your life. As you read this, there will be affirmations that I have listed you may want to use but also other affirmations will come to mind for you or you will find that some of the statements I make can be converted into affirmations. Affirmations are not just about changing our way of thinking so that we have less stress in our lives and better health and more joy, it is about changing the world. When we have a positive thought or a negative thought it affects us but it also goes out into the world as the energy that it is. If more and more people learn to use affirmations, affirmations will become that much more easy, effective, and life changing. We can truly make the world dramatically better and it can happen in a matter of a few years like a quantum leap.

Do you realize that authentic mindfulness leads to internal coherence? Mindfulness-based pedagogy, also known as affirmation-based pedagogy or compassion-based pedagogy, is the key to societal improvement because it involves a change in consciousness. At its most basic precept, it calls for educators to remove stress from their lives, their classrooms and schools by using affirmations such as the following:

I release the past and am grateful that it has brought me new awareness.

It is easy for me to make changes accordingly.

I feel good about myself as an educator.

I spend more time in my classroom.

I love getting positive e-mails from parents.

I love hearing good news from parents.

I love seeing my students happy.

I love laughing with my students.

I do not judge because I am non judging.

I am patient.

I am changing and growing through the challenges that come my way, I strive for the perfect classroom. I cloak my classroom in radiant light and love. I arm my classroom with peace and optimism. Only the best of myself is available to my students, co-workers, and administrators.

I am powerful.

I have energy in the class; I have increasing energy.

I have good posture in the class.

I am organized.

I am always on time.

I'm thankful for my students and co-workers.

I am confident; I exude confidence.

I am in the process of promotion and pay increase(s).

My classes are compliant, well behaved, submissive and enjoy and respect me as a teacher and I am grateful.

I am smart.

I look professional; I am professional; I am a professional.

I am an exemplary teacher.

I am assertive.

I am a star teacher.

I speak positively with others and listen with compassion.

I see with love and hear with compassion.

My career brings me great satisfaction.

I dispel laziness, both my own and my students'; I know laziness destroys, but I am smart enough to avoid it at all times.

Others treat me with respect.

I am the student whisperer.

Everything I touch is a success.

I am grateful for my career, students, ability to teach, classes, confidence, assertiveness, energy.

Blessings upon my classrooms.

Blessings and love vibrations upon my students.

My income is constantly increasing and so it should, for mine is the noblest of professions!

I love my job!

I go to the school whenever needed to work and remain focused on the task at hand.

'*So and so*' is the most improved student in the class…

I am truly grateful for the new people, circumstances, and events that are enhancing my career experience.

I take any jealousy directed by co-workers against me and convert that energy into making me more confident. I have a commanding presence/demeanor/energy in the classroom, staff room, and at meetings.

The computers at my school always work well for me. The photo-copier always works and always has paper. I get plenty notice of coverage of minutes and get along with all co-workers all of whom respect me.

All of my students want to learn, and so they listen, comply, respect me and are engaged in my lessons. Those who are defiant need to be corrected by their parents and I have the fortitude, courage and confidence to call parents accordingly and build parent-teacher relations.

I am attracting my ideal classroom.

I am clear about the type of classroom I want and know it is manifesting itself.

I am inspired. I get energy from inspiration, I especially use this energy at school. The inspiration in me relieves stress and impresses and attracts people.

I radiate a glow.

I harness energy in my classroom.

I vow to do all my marking within a week of getting it.

My students use my class website and/or Blackboard accordingly and appropriately.

I look forward to a productive day at work tomorrow.

I use a day plan.

I always feel appreciated at work.

I successfully partner between myself and parents.

I send home information bulletins or newsletters from time to time, telling about goals for specific projects, how various procedures are working in class and so on, and my Principal is impressed by how proactive I am.

I ask for parents' reactions and suggestions related to differentiated instruction.

I build partnerships with parents, just as I do with my students, to create a classroom in which individuals are honored and much is expected from every student.

Teaching is stressful for some or many but does not have to be for me. I realize that every complaint is an affirmation attracting into my life what I say I don't want and thus I catch myself when complaining and affirm: "That's the old me talking, I am safe, secure, and competent."

My students want to have me as a teacher again when done taking one of my courses.

I bring my awareness back to where it needs to be when I feel uncomfortable and thereby realize that I am at peace because I love my job.

My acceptance of my students is mirrored to me in every way.

Infinite wisdom and harmony reign supreme in my class.

My co-workers and I encourage each other and moreover our students.

I love my co-workers, students and administration; they all have my best interest at heart.

I have unlimited potential as a teacher and I convey this.

We will see other examples of affirmations later.

By the end of this book, you should have a new depth of understanding on affirmation based pedagogy whereby you are secure in the knowledge that both students and teachers can fast track to inner-peace like never before simply by using affirmations. This is because affirmations allow us to overcome our weaknesses circumventing the often ineffective "next steps" on report cards. As self-help author Dr. Bruce Lipton states: "...many of our strengths and weaknesses, the parts of ourselves we own as who we are, are directly attributable to familial and cultural perceptions downloaded into our minds before we were six years old. Programmed perceptions acquired in these developmental years are primarily responsible for health and behavioral issues experienced in our adult lives. Consider how many children never realize their full potential or dreams because of limiting programming." Now consider how many children can. This is why I was such a strong supporter of former Prime Minister of Canada, Paul Martin. His platform when he was running for re-election was to implement a full national childcare program so that pre-school children would be exposed to early childhood education environments as much as they needed. So many dysfunctional children from dysfunctional homes would literally behave and perform much better throughout school then they otherwise would because of the reduction in the cultural conditioning they were getting at home. Sadly, between him losing to Steven Harper and the economic collapse of 2009, it was no longer affordable. At least in Ontario, Premiere Dalton McGuinty introduced the extended Kindergarten program which was similar.

Naturally, not all school boards will be or are currently open to having anything to do with affirmations for various reasons but mostly because they fear flack from parents. Of course many parents will reject anything that comes along that they didn't have in schools when they were in school.

This negative thinking that 'if they didn't have it when they were young why do they need it now?' mentality can certainly be counter-productive. This can be irritating but understandable and should not be a case for boards to shun affirmations. To do so, would be fostering a negative affirmation on a grand scale. However, for boards that are right of center, and overly cautious (you can never be too cautious in the education business I suppose), they can at least incorporate student learning skills affirmations. Student learning skills affirmations are straight forward positive thinking in advance of exams, tests, and assignments (etc.). All school boards agree that students benefit from learning better study techniques and better note-taking methods. Basic affirmations can only help with this and in turn, also promote new brain pathways whereby students learn naturally that being a good learner involves feeling very confident about learning abilities. Our brains are designed to enjoy learning. A lot of teachers don't know that let alone our students. So many students have a negative view of themselves, and the more negative view of themselves the more they think they are poor learners and the more they think that the less likely they are to have a solid healthy positive rapport with their teacher(s). Affirmations can step in and fill voids. A student who thinks of themselves as a poor learner and they have an IEP (individual Education Plan for special needs students; affirmations in no way shape or form are meant to replace IEPs anymore than health affirmations are able to replace hospitals and doctors) might not even need an IEP if they use affirmations! So don't listen to affirmation nay-sayers in boards who say affirmation based pedagogy interferes with special education. However, an IEP that is followed + affirmations= even better results. Furthermore, many non-IEP students have a poor opinion of themselves too. We know this has a lot to do with their lack of confidence which has a lot to do with their home-life and self-image. Self-image affirmations and visualization will absolutely improve attitude, effort, participation, teamwork, and initiative. This is because the student in question changes their focus away from negative self-assessments. They develop the mindset of focusing on the kind of person they would like to be.

Students should be encouraged to surf the internet for affirmations for students, children, and/or teens on school-time and on their own time. They should be encouraged to journal write alongside this or at least write down affirmations they like and then begin writing their own. For example, the website "Teen Affirmations": http://www.self-help-and-self-development.com/teens_affirmations.html offers the following:

-Every day in every way I am getting better and better.

-My school is wonderful, my teachers are marvelous and my class mates are terrific.

-Studying comes easily to me and I love studying.

-I have a perfect memory and I can recall with ease.

-I concentrate easily and I am immune to distraction.

-I understand that habits make a person and I develop good habits.

And there are more to be found at that site and there are many others with more popping up on the world-wide-web every day.

Remember, when it comes to affirmations, it can be very tempting to abandon them when they don't work or the opposite of the affirmation in question transpires. So much of the literature that has been written about affirmations leaves out the part where they tell you that affirmations don't always work and why this is so and how to increase the frequency of them coming into fruition. *The Secret* is the most famous book ever written on the subject but I have always found it to come across as too good to be true in that it implies all that you have to do is think joyful thoughts and all your desires will come true. The first time I read the book, I got the impression I could win the lottery. However, in the sequel to *The Secret, The Power,* by Rhonda Byrne, you get an extensive explanation of all this. I can sum it up by saying that affirmations really don't work well as long as we are making negative affirmations and unfortunately, a lot of our negative affirmations don't register with us on a conscious level that they are in fact negative affirmations. The main example in *The Power* is saying "I'm fine" or "I'm OK" often which translates into a negative affirmation. Byrne put it this way: "...how do you know whether your thoughts are positive or negative? Your thoughts are positive when they are thoughts of what you want and love..." Man oh man alive, how many time have my thoughts been thoughts of what I don't love, like how stressful my job is or how much I didn't enjoy teaching ENG3C (Grade 11 College level English) or CH2P/L (Grade 10 Applied and Essential Life Skills Level Canadian History). If teachers are having thoughts like this and then off school-hours find themselves in a mall complaining about line-ups and poor service and price gouging, it all adds up to too many negative affirmations. The truth is affirmations work. Likewise, prayer works too but not everyone things so because of so-called unanswered prayers. So it is with affirmations. You have to believe. Also, joy is easy to come by but not everyone agrees with that based on their experiences. Anyone can experience joy. You simply can't be joyous and complain at the same time though. It's easy for teachers to find things to complain about but complaining is a waste of time since no good comes out of it. On the other hand, the opposite must be true that love attracts love. It was Jesus who said: "Then you will know the truth and the truth shall set you free." Subsequently, St.Paul said, "Love is the fulfilling of the law." So, affirmations do work, and when it seems they do not work, there is a reason for exactly why they are not working just like when a prayer seems to go unanswered. Prayer and affirmations go hand in hand. It is no wonder why all religions call for us to give love and to be charitable. *The Power* puts it this way: "...unless you give you will always be struggling to survive." So, don't make the same mistake I did and think that affirmations alone work, you need to give out in thought and deed for them to be fully activated. It's like that with prayer because prayers are affirmations. Oh, and you can never really truly give out love in thought and deed in full without being filled with thoughts of gratitude. Someone once said that "God helps those who help themselves." The problem with saying or thinking that is that it is a negative affirmation because it is both cynical and thankless.

Rhonda Byrne states that "Your work is meant to be exciting, and you are meant to accomplish all the things you would love to accomplish." That is an affirmation. You can put affirmations like this on your annual learning plan since the statement is especially true of teachers.

I am not a morning person. I never have been. I just said two negative affirmations. And because I have said them for most of my teaching career, I know one place where I have gone wrong. *The Power* tells us: "When you wake up each day, you should be filled with excitement because you *know* the day is going to be full of joy. You are meant to be laughing and full of joy. You are meant to be strong and safe." Gee, I can't count how many times I woke up and hit the snooze button (which as far as I can tell is NEVER a good thing), and thought to myself how horrendous the day was probably going to be or thought about how I was going to put up with *So and So's* nonsense today (So and So being a student(s) OR co-worker(s). *The Power* acknowledges that this is not as easy as just switching a switch in our minds to change, "...there will be challenges in your life, and you are meant to have them too, because they help you to grow, but you are meant to know how to overcome..." So I now know that affirmations involve a very positive approach to how we view the difficulties and bad luck that we encounter. I have had many bouts with bad luck where I have said "why me?" or I blamed God or thought that there was a vindictive student(s) out there putting hexes on me (of course if there was or is such a thing as hexes or "the evil eye," you would be protecting yourself by using affirmations). In the fall of 2010, my eleven-year-old 2001 Caviler was at 268,000 kilometers and I thought, and even had actual affirmations about it, that I would get one more winter out of it despite many people telling me over the last several years that this type of car is not a car that is designed to last past 200,000 clicks. And one night in October, it broke down. It overheated and no longer had the ability to contain engine coolant. I was so stressed-out and on the same night, I lost my cell phone (I should point out that I used to lose my cell phone almost weekly and used to hate myself literally for doing this or even felt rage against the universe for it happening so many times over and over again, however, I came to realize the meaning behind the expression "the absent minded professor" which I never realized referred to the idea that creative thinkers (and most teachers are naturally creative) have creative energy and are consequently naturally absent minded), my cell phone was also my only alarm clock and had the phone number for the supply teacher dispatch. So... a) I had no way of waking up on time the next day, b) no way of getting to school the next day and c) no way of calling in sick. I could feel the stress. I had a difficult time breathing properly. In the end, I got through it. My principal was very supportive as he always is. He gave my first class senior privileges, told me to rest and allowed me to take a personal day. Then came the buying of the new car and that was stressful for me because I did not have very much money or assets and was saving for my wedding which was less than a year away. Five days of stress had passed before I realized, the old car could very well have broken down on the way to school in the morning or in the middle of the night in the middle of nowhere or across the border several hours away from any friends or family or in the middle of harsh winter weather, or worse of all, right before the wedding. Hmmm.... Here's what's more interesting, I never really liked that old car even from the first day I bought it. And on top of that, I did often have thoughts of it breaking down on me. And in retrospect, it was unwise of me to let it get to 268,000 clicks. I didn't always hate my old car, but I surly never loved it. I do love my new Dodge Journey. And maybe it's a sign that it's called "Journey." Incidentally, A couple of weeks after I got it I did something called "Journey Work." It is a type of self-help counseling that I sought out to help with my issue of losing me keys, cell phone and other things so often. I have much more to say about bad luck in the luck chapter later in the book.

Love has more to do with affirmations than you can imagine, assuming that love is an extremely powerful and creative force, teachers, schools, books and education would not exist if it weren't for love. Positive affirmations thus work when we choose love. To use Christian terminology, we have to be teachers of the Beatitudes. Our attitude and our mindset must be love-based. This is when affirmations work. *The Power* states: "...you have a choice. You have a choice whether to love and harness the positive force- or not... a lack of love is the cause of all negative things and all the pain and suffering..." How many of those mornings when I have woken up feeling like I wanted nothing more than to go back to sleep did I think that I didn't want to go to work that day all because of one particular student or one particular co-worker or one particular class, or just feeling that the day was going to be stressful because I was so tired and/or disorganized? I certainly can look back and see how I attracted stress into my life.

In order to become good at affirmations, you must be mindful enough to recognize a negative affirmation when you hear one in the staff room. Here are some negative affirmations to avoid in the staff room:

-The staff room is full of spies anyway (I've heard this one. It means that you better be careful what you say because someone will repeat it to the principal).

-Administration won't do anything.

-That student is insane.

-This class is so loud they're going to give me a heart attack.

-The incident report form is a joke! (this one was a favorite of mine in 2009 when the Ontario Ministry of Education implemented safe school forms that a teacher had to full out and the principal would be obligated to act on, but the only incidents that you could use the forms for were weapons, drugs, and assault, the three things that it just so happens the students don't do, at least most of them don't, skipping school, swearing, chronic cell phone use, habitual neglect of homework or disruption of class seem to be fine, as long as nobody is high or drunk, carrying a weapon, or assaulting someone. But saying "it is a joke" is a negative affirmation. It would serve me better to say: "I am looking forward to the incident report and discipline system currently in place improving.").

I heard a colleague say once "I don't have to use my brain to teach this class" in reference to a particular group of students. Can you catch yourself when you laugh at a joke that is a negative affirmation? It's easier said than done. It takes practice but the benefits are undeniable.

In Ontario in 2010, the Ministry of Education eliminated term 1 report cards and replaced them with long-form progress-reports for all elementary schools. This in theory lessens a teacher's workload but more importantly it puts a greater emphasis on learning skills since we know that most parents and students care first and foremost about marks on a report card and not learning skills progression. In the Ottawa Catholic School Board, a brochure was sent home explaining the new system. In it was a chart called: "A Closer Look at Learning Skills and Work Habits." It talked about what constitutes responsibility, organization, independent work skills, collaboration skills, initiative, and self-regulation. Notice, that these are the building blocks of all affirmations. And what was especially progressive and mindful of this school board was a column put in the chart titled, "What a student might say or do to demonstrate this Learning Skill or Work Habit." They didn't use the word affirmation but they were all awesome affirmations. Some examples:

-I participate in classroom and group discussions by speaking and listening in turn

-I say please and thank you and use other language appropriate in my school

-I have all the materials I need

-I know how long the task will take. I can make a plan for learning

-I listen and speak respectfully

-I use words, actions, and images that respect others

-I ask questions to make sure I understand

-I know what I do well and what steps I need to take to improve.

-I check back to make sure I can meet my goals.

This book is more about affirmations that we as teachers can say but the easiest and best affirmations a student can say are those that are taken directly from the comment box of a report card or progress report. Many of them can be quickly helpful for a month or so and then no longer be needed and others can become life-long helpful affirmations. If you were to ask me what the most important affirmation a student can make was, I would say: "I am calm, focused, and alert." That's a good one for anyone of course but I say this because of what all the brain research tells about all learners and their brains and learning. Let me explain. Malcolm Gladwell put the marshmallow test, from forty years ago, on the map, when he referenced it, whereby seventy percent of children ate a marshmallow even though they were told that if they could resist eating the one in front of them for fifteen minutes they could have two. Even less of our students today have self-discipline skills levels that are capable of leading to the success in life they seek. The same marshmallow experiment was referenced a couple years later in 2010 Volume 12, Issue 2 edition of "People for Education Newsletter" to help show that students are best ready to learn when they are calmly focused and alert. So are less than twenty-five percent of your students meeting their full potential? Impaired cognitive performance is always present when a student is under stress or has not had enough sleep. Now, that same issue reported on a study that came up with six things that parents can do to increase their children's chances of success academically any of which can be converted into affirmations that parents can use and I have done that for you below:

1. I tell my son/daughter that it means a lot to me when s/he does well in school

2. I talk to my son/daughter about school

3. I read to my son/daughter and will continue to for as long as I need to

4. I go to concerts and sporting events with him/her

5. I go over my son/daughter's/children's report card with him/her/them

6. I always go to parent interviews

It makes perfect sense, I teach about sixty-five students a semester and on parent interview night, I will get about eight or nine interviews! And those students almost always notice their marks go up in the following term. One thing is for sure, these six steps of mindfulness are a solid path to improved attendance, student engagement and positive relationships. Students will be happier, plain and simple.

We need to use affirmations to: focus awareness, increase our energy levels, lower our stress levels, help our students improve attention, promote academic achievement, reduce problem behaviors, increase enthusiasm for learning, develop a deeper understanding of student motivation and engagement, strengthen critical and creative thinking, and foster more self-directed learners.

I close this chapter with the most well written employment affirmation I think has ever been written. It comes from *Meditations to Heal Your Life* by Louise L. Hay:

> As I employ my Higher Self, my Higher Self employs me. What a wonderful, brilliant, delicate, strong, beautiful energy my inner spirit is. It blesses me with fulfilling work. Each day is new and different. As I let go of the struggle to survive, I find that I am fed, clothed, housed, and loved in ways that are deeply fulfilling to me. I make it okay for me and others to have money without working hard at a job. I am worthy of bringing in good money without struggling in the rat race or fighting traffic. I follow my higher instincts and listen to my heart in all that I do.

CHAPTER 2

LEADERSHIP

If you are called to be a teacher, you are called to model behavior. To do this one must be a leader. What words come to mind when you hear the word leader? Hopefully, one of the words is "conviction." With conviction, a lot of things fall into place naturally.

A good starting point is to affirm for yourself that you are a good leader. In *Healing the Hardware of the Soul,* best-selling author Daniel G. Amen uses brain research to reveal two types of leaders, negative (with poor planning skills) and positive. He states: "A teacher with poor planning skills will teach the bare minimum and does not adequately prepare students for the next step in their education. A healthy brain even after the age of thirty when the brain plateaus, remembers things accurately and effectively. This is a key part of being an organized teacher. On the other hand, memory problems can occur if a brain is not kept in shape thereby impairing teachers as they may forget important information to teach or in the case of coaching, ignore important trends that are happening in a game." As you will see we can use affirmations to have the best planning skills possible.

Now you may think, this is all well and good, but like all professional development, how practical is it when you get a class from Hell? We will deal with this in the chapter entitled: "ENG3C"

It's finally happening: schools and school boards are offering professional-development workshops dealing with brain research. But what's needed now is the same dedication to affirmations. Long before *The Secret* was published, the late Norman Vincent Peale and Louise Hay were writing many books on the power of positive thinking. Although this is a philosophy that is ancient, not until the twentieth century (with new medical and scientific understandings to go along with it), has it become practical. William James once said: "The greatest discovery of my generation is that human beings can alter their lives by altering their attitudes." Now as any educator knows, education has not changed in real terms in 100 years. Go ahead and Google images of classrooms from 1800, 1900, 2000. They all pretty much look the same. About every ten years, pedagogy changes, curriculum changes, technology changes (etc.), to a certain extent, but essentially, the drop-out rate, the suspension rate, the teacher burn-out rate is the same. Imagine education taking a quantum leap forward. We can flush out all the old ways of thinking. We can fill our minds and thus our classrooms with fresh, new, creative thoughts of faith, love and goodness. By this process, we can remake our schools and educational institutions. What we need to do is teach ourselves and our students to imagine what they want to be habitually.

Have we not been saying to our students for 100 years: "You can do anything you set your mind to" and "don't let anyone tell you you can't accomplish a goal"? Yet, by the time students are in Kindergarten do we not already have them pegged as university, college, or workplace students? We usually do. A teacher of any grade can look at vocabulary/literacy, academic history, social ineptness, and family life and know fairly accurately what path the student is on. If we taught our students, but also ourselves, because it has to start with us- that positive thoughts create around us an atmosphere propitious to the development of positive outcomes, the positive change would happen overnight. We know the opposite is true of negative thoughts and yet bullying, for example, is as alive and well as it always has been. There is a public perception that teachers don't do anything about it. Zero tolerance policies have failed. Permissive restorative-justice measures have failed even more so (for example, a student steals my MasterCard and spends $3,000 and instead of my pressing charges, which is what I would have to do to get the credit-card company to refund me, I sit down with the student and a third party (typically a councilor), and I state how I forgive him/her, and we all feel warm and fuzzy afterward. I don't know about you, but I want my $3,000 back). In reality, there is a time and place for restorative justice, and the need for a zero tolerance argument could be eliminated through implementing of changing our thoughts and learning to control our egos. It's not as if nobody has ever done this. Some of the most successful people to ever walk the face of the earth did just this. Humans, especially young students passively accept unsatisfactory circumstances. Imagine an interdisciplinary course on how to think where thirty students have a final exam question, "Define 'law of prosperity'" and the students all know to write, "Believe and succeed." That's thirty students who have increased their odds of success or who have reduced the amount of suffering and sacrifice they will need to undergo to obtain inner peace in their lives. They would automatically evolve their own leadership skills as well.

When I think of true leadership I think of self-love as a necessary component. Most people do not love themselves. Some people stop loving themselves in childhood and some in their teen years and there are those who don't until they are adults. But clearly, just because you do not love yourself doesn't mean it always must be this way. If we understand that when we love ourselves, we can't hurt ourselves or others and we don't attract negative events into our lives, then we can be true leaders and model true leadership. Teachers who love themselves will encounter far less issues in the classroom. Here's the tricky part: We can't love ourselves and blame ourselves for mistakes at the same time. We can't love ourselves and imagine what people are saying behind our backs. It's one or the other. Either one takes very little effort. When we catch ourselves calling ourselves stupid for a mistake(s), say to yourself, "Whoa. I am a teacher, I know the value in learning, I learn from each and every mistake, I thus release the need to be mad at me or anyone else and I love myself." This is a great affirmation. Most affirmations should be short and sweet. But some can be a paragraph. That last one was a mouthful I know, but I am confident it is worth it and that it works. Try it. Another way to put it, to quote Louise Hay from the book *Inner Wisdom-Meditations for the Heart and Soul*, "...I am willing to stop punishing me for my mistakes. Instead, I love myself for my willingness to learn and grow."

We want our principals to be good leaders but the truth is they are not perfect. Don't make the same mistake I did at one point early in my career where I literally despised my principal. It is never ever worth it. Trust me!

The Power puts it best by teaching us that "If you think, "I can't stand my boss," that thought is expressing a strong negative *feeling* you have about your boss, and you're giving out that negative feeling. As a consequence, your relationship with your boss will continue to get worse."

Remember I said that there is a time and place for restorative justice? Well, the last thing I want to say about leadership is that being a leader involves disciplining subordinates when applicable. A good leader disciplines effectively. A good leader also knows that anyone who is disciplined under their command will not improve their behavior if discipline is the only form of one-on-one communication going on. In *The Little Book of Restorative Discipline for Schools- Teaching Responsibility; creating caring climates* by Lorraine Stutzman Amstunys and Judy H. Mullet, it is well put: "Discipline from a restorative perspective may be compared to a checking account. If you take money out and make no deposits, you become bankrupt. When a child is disciplined, a withdrawal is made on the *relationship* account. The relationship account itself is based on respect, mutual accountability, and even friendship established within a caring community. If the substrata work of community-building has not been done, the child is bankrupt and has nothing to lose by misbehaving or by being confronted. The child's motivation to change is limited." It is a scary thought to have a student in your class who feels s/he has nothing to lose! The solution according to the book I have just quoted is affirmations: "...a teacher would need to provide five affirmations for each confrontation." Therefore, a good affirmation would be to say often: "I am open to restorative justice strategies and I provide at least five compliments to a student who I have to discipline." You might feel that the student does not deserve praise but in this case it does not matter, you would be selfish not to and stubborn since the complimenting will maximize the sticking of the discipline. Remind yourself that you are a leader and are above egotistical reactionary thinking. The bottom line here is that punishing students who you have a difficult time bringing yourself to like and not praising will ensure that they keep on their path of misbehavior. It will not lessen your stress to look for ways to punish them. Looking for ways to praise them will always motivate them and as is stated in *It's the Thought That Counts* by David R. Hamilton, "When a person is highly motivated, genes switch on, brain cells grow..." Wow! Imagine at the end of your career the feeling of accomplishment knowing that you have contributed to multiple students maximizing their brain development! If you teach college or university, you may be tempted to think that it is too late by the time a student gets to you to change their behavior. It is a logical assumption but it turns out to be wrong. Hamilton goes on to state: "Everyone can live their dreams, regardless of past conditions or the performances of family members."

CHAPTER 3

VISUALIZING SUCCESS

I have never heard of a teacher using "visualizing" as a next step on a report card maybe because the principal would not recognize it as acceptable for a report card comment box but for the most part, we have not considered it. I am on the joint PD committee in my board (joint as in made up by the board and the union) and a year before this book was written there was a survey of all teachers about PD, and not one teacher in 1000 mentioned anything about affirmations. There were a couple superintendents that briefly mentioned affirmations at PD days around the same time which was very proactive to see in my opinion. But it's true, if our students visualized, there would be more success. Maybe we should be using it as a report card comment. Imagine when you died, you were given a report card written by God. What would it say? What expectations would you have met? There would be a box for relationships, one for health, one for finances which would have three strands, one of which would be charity, and one box would be your career. Mine might read like this: "Rob demonstrates some knowledge and understanding of the concepts of the universe and to a satisfactory degree, has applied this with a generally good effort in his career. A poor test result has hindered his mark. Rob was encouraged to seek clarification and extra assistance when needed but did not always do this. Rob was also encouraged to ensure his communication with students, colleagues, administrators, and parents was professional, timely, and proactive and he generally met these expectations sometimes with attention to quality and detail. He has demonstrated a good understanding of the skills and concepts that he taught his students. He regularly volunteered to go beyond his job description to maintain rapport with those he encountered. He usually came to class on time and with care, ready to work. He could have benefitted by applying more effort and energy to reducing his tendency to complain about things in general which impeded his preparation time. Rob self-advocated when he was in need of assistance. To his credit, he was eager to learn, however, he often expected his students to have a positive attitude towards learning in times when he himself did not. He accepted responsibility for his own behavior. He went on to develop positive work habits and utilized organizational tools in positive ways. He was a man of faith and this showed to his students. He approached activities with a positive attitude. By the end of his life, he could accurately explain the local, global, and national forces that had helped to shape the education system during his lifetime."

Visualizing is all about moving forward. A lot of people consider themselves optimistic but really aren't because they do not visualize their optimism. Visualizing success must involve optimism and vice versa. In the 2010 spring edition of *Canadian Health and Lifestyle* magazine, it reads: "Although sometimes difficult to see the silver lining in a dark cloud, looking for the positives goes a long way towards moving forward. When children see and hear you making positive predictions about your future, they're inclined to do the same." By the way that is taken from an article that lists optimism as one of the ten key traits that a parent should have but obviously any trait a parent should have so to a teacher, so I have taken those ten and made them into an affirmation: I display traits of perseverance, fairness, courage, honesty, integrity, optimism, respect, responsibility, initiative, and empathy.

There is nothing more important than visualizing success. Without visualizing, affirmations are not as effective. Just as a negative affirmation can be reworded into a positive one, when you verbalize a goal or potential good idea and do not follow through, it becomes a negative affirmation.

Something as simple as visualizing achievement is powerful, and yet teachers tend to do the opposite. How many teachers get their teaching assignment for the next year and feel as if they have been demoted even though they are still teaching what they are qualified to teach and have not taken a pay cut?

Or how many look at their class list for the upcoming school year and feel defeated because of all the infamous names that appear on it. Some teachers think, "It will be all behavior management and no curriculum." I know I have. There is a vortex of a harmonious teaching that you are far from when thinking these thoughts. You would think that such teachers can never be master teachers though they are well within their rights to think the way they do, aren't they? Assuming you believe that we as humans are entitled to certain things. One could argue however that feeling entitled to things gets in the way of mindfulness. In fact, the most popular complaint I have made or heard about students is their sense of entitlement. These teachers in question can of course be master teachers- they simply have to be less cynical and take creative control of their own thoughts and expectations. They, like our students, need to take responsibility for their own happiness in life. An influx of new thoughts can be a great makeover. If you speak hopefully about all your students, that's the way you will think and your students will love you as a teacher. But as a teacher, you always need to be firm and assertive. When I was at my beginning teachers' orientation, the director of the school board at the time said, "They have to hate you a little before they love you a lot" (Greg McNally). This is wise and true. You need separate affirmations for the first day of school to be sure.

We will talk in detail about stress later in the book but visualizing around stress is a way to block stress, especially for teachers. Teachers sometimes get their priorities mixed up and this can cause stress. Visualizing can deal effectively with this issue. Stress is fear. Sometimes we set ourselves up as teachers. We cannot be at peace with ourselves (you can't have peace and be stressed at the same time) if we for example, neglect our day plan, or speed mark an exam(s) or culminating task(s) or do report cards or annual learning plans at the last minute. Affirm: I visualize more and more success in my classroom and school; I am a capable person who is centered and focused and so I am serine in any situation.

When I think of every union meeting I have ever led I think of some of the group discussions and they have often focused on something negative; complaining about something and/or anticipating worsening working conditions. There is not a whole lot of visualizing success going on. And at staff meetings when there are student and teacher success segments we tend to think "Oh boy, here we go, what a waste of time." But maybe we should consider what *The Power* has to say about this: "If you think, "I work with some fabulous people in my job," those words are expressing the positive feeling you have about the people you work with and you're giving out that positive feeling." Come to think of it, I am very thankful that over the last decade I have had exemplary teachers who are smart, funny, supportive, thoughtful, and inspiring, to work with. I have no reason to complain about any of them. That was just an affirmation.

Positive visualizing can lead to mind-over matter in our lives. In the book *It's the Thought That Counts- Why Mind Over Matter Really Works,* author Dr. David R. Hamilton , states, "...our thoughts and feelings, ideas and beliefs, and hopes and dreams alter the condition of our bodies, the circumstances of our lives, and even the state of the world." Visualizing events can predict the future in our lives and we can choose these images to be positive or negative. Our imagination helped us experience joy when we were children and it can do the same for us now. Hamilton explains it, "Molecules known as neuropeptides link our thoughts and emotions to every part of our bodies." You are what you visualize. Hamilton's book has a chapter called "The Power of Intention" where he proves the benefits of combining visualization and affirmations. For instance, "Scientific journals contain hundreds of research papers that show that we can use mental techniques to affect both our own bodies and those of other people." We as teachers, affect students all the time. Let's make these effects all positive. It will require us to be as compassionate as possible but studies show that compassion boosts the immune system so maybe instead of thinking that being more compassionate is more work, we should think of it more in terms of us getting more results from our students and at the same time getting less colds and flus during our career. Speaking of which, I had a co-worker write on the white-board in the staffroom one day: "Untreated, the common cold takes seven days to get over, and with treatment it takes a week." I can't say I mind the jab at the pharmaceuticals but I also can't say I agree with this statement since affirmations can override statistics. We all know what the placebo effect is but Hamilton refers to what he calls "the nocebo effect" (i.e. when we believe that it isn't possible for an illness to disappear right away). There have been cases of people who wear glasses who wake up one day and have improved eyesight and no longer need glasses! We have to visualize, we have to affirm what we visualize, we have to have intention, we have to believe in our visualizations.

CHAPTER 4

ENG3C

It is not enough to just visualize. We have to know why our students are behaving the way they are. If most of them are thinking negative thoughts or are angry we have to be mindful that their heart is physically and literally beating differently than people who are thinking positive thoughts or thoughts of appreciation. This chapter is named after one of my worst teaching experiences. If you are a teacher who never has behavior problems you may find some of this chapter non-applicable. However, most of you have imagined what it is like to teach in a classroom where there are no behavior issues. And when we visualize this life, would we not breath more easily, sleep better, walk differently (what I mean by that is walk with superior confidence. I have a close friend who is an excellent teacher and long before he was ever a teacher, I used to always tell him that he had a "VP Walk." He in turn knew what I meant, that he walked like my vice-principal used to walk when I was in high school), perhaps talk differently and react differently? I would say yes, because we would feel different. We would be relaxed. The problem is that I know too many teachers over the age of fifty who still haven't got that fantasy teaching schedule. The other problem is we sometimes get a class that we think is beyond anything we have ever had to manage and we think that once the semester is over we will not have to face such a challenging group again. Maybe that is true, but not in my case and not in most cases.

As I write this, I have taught ten years full time and my most brutal class in terms of disturbing behavior was one particular group of grade eleven students. The class was Grade 11 College level English, ENG3C.

You can't be a teacher and not deal with conflicts. When you have a student that is beyond difficult and seems like an exception to the rule and you can't quite bring yourself to be as sympathetic to him/her as you should, it is time to do something about it, perhaps involve a third party like a principal, parent, student-support worker, or other teacher (we are a team after all). Of course the situation is dependent upon that third party also being gifted or versed in positive thinking. There will always be negative people (this is true since even the most positive people are negative sometimes) and thus negative students. Do not abandon your negative students any more than you would your co-workers, friends, or family when any of them are being negative. If you try everything and June rolls around and the student is worse not better, it may be grounds for the student to be removed from the classroom in which case the log documentation should clearly back this up. However, in most cases, you in turn are offering students your thought patterns without taking their negativism, and as for your fellow positive students, co-workers, friends, and family, the more of these the better. The more you can harness their energy, just the way a rock star does as he/she walks on stage and 20,000 people are sending that one person solid, vital, positive vibes mixed with love, enthusiasm, and gratitude, the better.

Now I am not delusional. I know teachers are not rock stars, but students look forward to rock concerts don't they? These concerts they are attending involve them knowing ahead of time that they will enjoy it. Students can develop a love of learning and thus look forward to learning. So, when you enter your classroom, don't expect them to cheer and applaud (although that would be nice), but expect them to be smiling and ready to learn as opposed to bored, tired, uninterested and asking if they can watch a movie or go outside for class. They still might ask those questions though, and although it is insulting it may be because their other classes are not as positive as yours and they feel stressed anyway.

So would I teach ENG3C again by choice? Probably not. Was I assigned to teach the same group the following year (ENG4C)? Yes. Now it may be because of the law of attraction in my not thinking about not wanting it, it may be a coincidence, it may be the principal purposely assigning it to me because he wanted to schedule other teachers in the department ahead of me first because he deems them more qualified in terms of their credentials thereby giving me the 'left-overs', or maybe the universe is telling me that I need to teach them again to practice what I preach. All I know is when I first was given the teaching assignment I felt like crying. My first thought was "FML." But I changed my thinking. By the way, speaking of "FML" it is obvious that students use these new Facebook/MSN abbreviations constantly now and as a matter of fact, FML is a negative affirmation. And now we teachers are starting to use these ourselves. For those of you that have no idea what FML stands for, one of your affirmations may need to look at being in touch with youth; it stands for "Fuck my life."

Always keep in mind the law of attraction when you have a difficult group of students. If you have a difficult class and are jealous or resentful of a co-worker who has what appears to be a dream schedule (perhaps they have Prep first period, a second Prep period designated as a dean, attendance officer, student success supporter, or differentiated instruction coach, followed by Grade 12 University level English with nine students and last period of the day is spent supervising students in the library as they work on-line), you are making sure that you won't be attracting any sort of a dream schedule anytime soon. Therefore, any time you hear of another teacher receiving more of what they want, get excited and be happy for them. By doing this, you have nothing to lose, by not doing it, you are adding to your workload this year, and the year after that, and the year after that.

I look back and know that at the end of that ENG3C class, although it could have been a much more pleasant experience for everyone involved, in the end, the stress didn't matter. At the end, I had reestablished rapport that was lost. But we should never lose rapport to begin with. The best way to keep rapport I now find is to always have compassion for all your students. If you are a first year teacher, don't let it take ten years to realize this. If we call a student 'bad', as I'm sure most of us have, we are thinking of them as bad and according to the law of attraction, we have labeled ourselves as bad.

At the beginning of this chapter I talked about hearts beating differently. The term for this is internal coherence. We need to want for ourselves and for our students, a state where our hearts beat smooth, whereby our immune system is at its best and our mindset is positive. In *It's The Thought That Counts* we learn that "In further investigating the effects on the heart, scientists at the University of Utah published a study in 2006 demonstrating that a hostile attitude could cause heart disease. The study involved 150 married couples between the ages of 60 and 70 and found that where the women were openly hostile, making statements such as, "You can be so stupid sometimes," there was a greater amount of hardening of their arteries; and when men were more controlling, making statements such as "I'll do what you want to get you off my back," then there was more hardening in *their* arteries." The same author goes on to talk about the health benefits of laughing. I can honestly say that my students often laugh in my class and it is great but I recall my ENG3C class not laughing most days or when they did it was not for appropriate reasons and therefore not genuine humor.

As for my ENG3C class, they went on to become my ENG4C class. I was mindful enough to try new things with them. For example, as an English teacher, I now know I can use poetry to get students to meditate through writing. In the May/June 2010 edition of *Ki Awareness* Magazine, there is an article called "Positivity Finding Through Poetry" by Michael Joseph (he is the co-founder of Pillars of Positivity) where he says: "… the poetic process has opened up so many possibilities to teach the art of positive living to both adults and children. Poetry provides a unique experience of self healing and expression. It is one of the many ways we can allow ourselves the unique ability to achieve self-actualization on a daily basis." Poetry does not require the writer to be a gifted writer. Students like to get creative and when they are creative they have less stress and are more likely to turn negative emotions into positive ones. You see I did know this when I taught my ENG3C class but I made the mistake of blaming the students for their lack of interest and work-ethic. So yes, my ENG4C class was a million times better an experience than my ENG3C and that same semester I had a huge CH2P/L (Canadian History, Grade ten applied and essential level combined) that was far more needy and challenging than my ENG3C class and it too went well in that a) the students progressed well at their ability to focus, difficult thought it was, b) the parents were mostly supportive which makes such a difference and c) I complained far less about my CH2P class than I did my 3C class even though the 2P class was far more needy and far more challenging. Mind you, I was very disturbed by some very dark behavior in that class and was very disturbed at the glaring lack of consequences for some serious behavior. I once said to the vice principal "as per progressive discipline, I suggest a suspension" in reference to a grade ten girl who lit a piece a paper on fire and gave a boy in the class a black eye and the vice-principal got her back up a little bit by replying, "I know all about how progressive discipline works so you don't have to worry about that just so you know." I accepted that because I mindfully thought that she took offense to something I said where no offense was meant. I can see how she would infer that I thought I knew more about the concept than she did. That was not my intention and I let it go. I could have used more mindful phrasing to be sure. Why do administrators sometimes not discipline students? Well, for the same reason as teachers since they themselves used to be teachers. I recall going home that day in question feeling over-tired, stressed, angry, offended, and with a slight headache. Most of my anger was directed at the administration and the system. My day was positive right up until the last hour in that building. From two-o'clock PM to about five-thirty PM, I was thinking of nothing else. When we do this as teachers, we are dwelling on something negative about or job. This is normal because out-of-control behavior is usually unpleasant and difficult to forget about. But in thinking about it, it is likely that we are actually helping to build new cells with a memory for dysfunctional encounters. Our mental images and their associated feelings of gloom will switch on specific genes that build up diseased cells in our bodies. That day in question was a Friday afternoon. Later that weekend I went to a wellness-spa and had my first ion-cleanse de-tox.

Scientists have done studies on rats where rats deprived of physical contact with their mother have very different behavior and health than the regular rats. I feel sad that I have not felt more sympathy in the past for habitual behavior-problem students like those in 3C and 2P who I know had a depressing home-life in comparison to the their classmates and other friends. These scientists found that deprivation of touch has a stunning effect on growth. It's true, most of my behavior-problem students have been short. I, myself, though having the greatest mother in the world who gave me more than enough support, affection, love, and attention, am short. My mother had post-partum depression when I was first born and I was not with her for the first several weeks or months and genetically I had not tall grand-parents, so alas, I am short. So I need to affirm that I have more sympathy for my students. Of course, this does not justify their behavior. I will just have more energy in dealing with said behavior.

On days when nothing seems to work and you feel like yelling at your students (which you can't do of course), remind yourself of this very handy and effective affirmation: "The Power of the Universe backs me in all of my endeavors, and I have boundless energy to get things done easily and quickly. Joy is certainly a motivator." -Louise Hay-.

CHAPTER 5

LET THE DEAD REST

As you can tell by the Shakespearian title of this chapter, it has to do with how we view the past. Viewing it in an over-negative or over-positive way can hold us back. Sometimes, teachers talk about the past and view it as a housing a better education system than today's. What do you believe? That may be right on some levels, to a certain extent. It can, however, be counter-productive if in our thoughts we are dismissing the current system. Teachers cannot be master-teachers if they are cynical, remember this. I remember when I was in Teachers College doing my placement, my supervisor said, "The kids never change." There were times in my career when I couldn't have disagreed more, but in hindsight, he was right.

Educator and brain researcher, Dr. Kathie F. Nunley states in *Differentiating the High School Classroom* that we must start to see "the good old days are now." She says, "The rumours that there was once a time when teachers felt that the majority of their students came well prepared and ready to learn, when one teaching method fit the needs of every learner in the room, are just that- rumours." Unfortunately, there are some current systems that are grossly flawed making it hard to resist cynicism. For example, while his heart might be in the right place, Obama's thinking that longer school days and longer school years and merit pay are steps in the right direction is as mistaken as Bush's "no child left behind." In Ontario, Canada, in 1997, teachers rightfully went on strike (the largest strike in North American history), when former Premiere Mike Hariss closed schools, fired teachers, slashed funding on a grand scale and drastically changed the system, one that has not yet recovered. And today, the province's post-secondary education facilities are scratching their heads over why the Ministry of Education is encouraging high schools to inflate marks and pass all students. There's an unfortunate "ignore the problem and it will go away" pedagogy in place for some reason I have spent over nine years trying to figure out. Recently, a board consultant said at a workshop on assessment and evaluation that "incompletes" (work that was never handed in) ought not count against the student since the work not handed in reflects expectations that are tested in other assignments anyway. To put this in perspective, she said, "When I was in university, I would have four or five essays in one course, and they were all testing the same expectations, so really, I didn't need to do all of them..." This may sound absurd. I know I don't agree but it does me no good to disagree and do nothing other than complain about a system. And it certainly does the system no good. I also need to try and understand all the sides. I need to affirm that I make it a routine to do so. There is a logic to the other side's argument, there has to be for it to be policy. It increases the students chance of passing and does not harm their self-esteem but the problem is that it is a negative affirmation. Students who would normally fail but always pass will learn they can't succeed on their own. Why is the school year ten months long if all those formative assignments have no value? The Ministry of Educations in this province and many other provinces and states are somewhat obsessed with more instructional time and less non-academic time; this is my favorite! It's laughable to think that less non-academic time is beneficial. You can literally feel the learning at some assemblies. The best ones cost money, so perhaps it's a hidden agenda to cut costs. As I said, I have not figured it out. Maybe I will never figure it out, but I know the system does not work well enough, and thankfully it is obviously inevitable that the system will change or is changing. It may take activist teachers for this to fully come into fruition. Thus, regardless of the system, it is always a smart decision to be optimistic, secure in the knowledge that the system will improve.

For the record, long before I was a teacher I knew that school spirit levels correlate with academics. If the students are attending extra-curricular events in droves, the school will produce greater achievement. But there will always be those who are convinced that we need more instructional time; some would get rid of Student Councils altogether. Indeed, students are getting more time to be unengaged, off task, and more time to not fit in the classroom.

The bad news for teachers isn't that students are more unengaged, it is as the book *The Power* describes: "…when you think or discuss negative things about someone else, you're sticking those negative things to you too, and you're putting them into your life." All the more reason for teachers to be mindful since we have to engage in report card comments, behavior logs and behavior management, discussions on union issues (etc). So let's be mindful in our thoughts and in the staff room that we don't bash and insult some of our more defiant pupils because it is not worth it. The author of *The Power,* Rhonda Byrne puts it best by saying: "…if you stick a label on any person… you are sticking the label on you, and that's what you will receive." We have to be careful because it is in our nature to label students. This is really the hardest part of the job. Byrne probably did not have teachers in mind, at least not specifically, when she said, "…if you *negatively* affect another person so much that the person goes on to negatively affect someone else, then the negativity will return to you in full. You will receive it back in the form of negative circumstances affecting money, your career, your health, or your relationships." Yet, as teachers, we are constantly put in a position where we have to scrutinize a student's work or discipline a student. What are our thoughts when we are in these moments?

Something like staff room gossip on the other hand, that can easily be eliminated. Even, if you are addicted to gossip, you can quickly program yourself to avoid it. *The Power* puts this in perspective: "…we need to be mindful of not sticking our nose in other people's business, because their business will get stuck in our nose!" Now, you might say, "But I just sit in the staff room minding my own business and people always make comments about other staff members and I can't control that." Actually, I believe that you can notice a decline in gossip at your school if you deflect by saying something like "I see your point about so-and- so but at the end of the day, I like having him/her as a co-worker." If the co-worker is complaining about the principal you can come back with pointing out something that you like about the principal. However, you do not want to make the mistake I used to always make and say, "The devil you know is better than the devil you don't know" or "You don't know how good you got because my last principal was so unfair that there is no comparison!" Here, you defeat the purpose by adding negative statements and you also risk trivializing what your co-worker may be dealing with. In any event, be aware that "gossip is giving negativity and that's exactly what you receive back" (*The Power*).

No matter what we say or think of the previous systems, we know how much bullying and gossiping and behavior issues there are in all schools and thus need to affirm strongly that this is finally changing. No matter what we say or think of the previous systems we know how noble professions that save and enhance lives and make the world a better a place have been populated by alumni that have been taught by good teachers in good schools and we need to affirm strongly that this will continue to happen even more so.

CHAPTER 6

DIFFERENTIATE

Over the last couple of years, the vast majority of professional development I have been exposed to has been based around differentiated instruction. This is a wonderful initiative since it is a reflection that the education system is concerned with what recent brain research has proven about learning.

Differentiating is important. The more you differentiate instruction, the more learning takes place in your class, the more learning taking place in your class, the more positive energy you will have as a teacher, the more positive energy you have, the less behavior problems you will attract. Make sense? It makes sense to make affirmations about differentiating. If you use assistive technology, word walls, develop lesson plans that address the needs of all types of learners (audio, visual, tactile), and keep your lessons original and current, you are doing a great deal of differentiating thereby increasing students' attentiveness and effort. It's actually quite easy. Most of us do not do enough of it in the classroom even though we constantly intend to. Affirmations are perfect for making things that are supposed to be easy, easy. Dieting should be easy for example but is so challenging for millions of us. People who combine dieting with affirmations find how much easier it is. So too, combining differentiating instruction as a strategy with affirmations is even more conducive to pro-active energy in the classroom. I am confident of this. Just because you work in a board or a school that is not progressive in terms of professional development, does not mean your classroom can't be progressive in this way.

Differentiating the classroom to meet all learning styles and keeping yourself and your students in a positive mindset is what is most conducive to long-term learning or to an increased ability to transfer that knowledge to other situations. Without positive attitudes, what good is Blooms Taxonomy or "layered curriculum"? Without joyous empowered teachers and students, no pedagogy or technology will meet the needs of all the students. Mindfulness is more than just a tool.

We of course need constant professional development. And we need to always think about strategies that work for us and our rapport with students and the school itself. For example, some school boards require their teachers to maintain an Annual Learning Plan. This lists professional goals, strategies, activities, and development, outlining what the teacher is doing and plans to do to be an effective teacher. I always put a lot of effort into my ALP and update it throughout the year. My principal told me one year that mine was the most extensive on the staff (which is great but you don't want to have an overwhelming amount of information on it). You may not want to hear that, because teachers often get their back up when they perceive another teacher to imply that they are bragging. Or if they perceive that you are somehow suggesting that you are a better teacher than they are. Intentional bragging is a negative affirmation but so is inferring false assumptions. The truth is most teachers just throw something generic together, save it, and press "print" every September. This does not necessarily reflect laziness on the part of the teacher if the administration does not look these over closely every year. Then again, it can reflect at the very least, procrastination. However, one could argue that if you don't have your energy level at its optimum output in September you're setting yourself up for mediocrity. Therefore, putting off your ALP can be a very negative affirmation. So much of the affirmations we make in late August and early September set the tone for the year. So as a teacher, this is the most important time of the year for affirmation diligence. So do not make the mistake of slacking-off when it comes to your ALP. It is potentially a similar mistake to getting through to June and figuring that you just need to coast along for the final three and a half weeks. Many a principal can attest that there are typically more unhappy students and parents in June than any other month. We need to precondition our students' minds to success and we need energy for this. We need to give energy to get energy. So, this is our chance.

This is all about teaching success. Do we even teach what success is in real terms? If most students associate the word with money, then the answer is, probably not. It's not about achievement so much as it is about handling your life effectively/efficiently whereby you are a creative individual. True confidence is one true source of happiness.

Speaking of energy, all teachers have experienced that feeling of walking into the staff room at the end of the day and plopping down on the couch ready to sleep for weeks because they are so tired they can't see straight. I've had this happen many times and I've even called in sick from fatigue. Some boards would deduct a day's pay for that and although I do not agree with that philosophy, I can understand the idea that if you are too tired to teach it is not the same thing as getting a flu virus that you had no choice in preventing. You could have a medical condition known as chronic fatigue syndrome, but for the purpose of this discussion we are not counting that since it does not apply to 99% of the fatigue we teachers deal with. Norman Vincent Peale talked about a "first layer of fatigue." He talked about untapped sources of power that we all have access to. He illustrates in all his books that the prerequisite is to recondition our minds.

When we are tired, we tend to cover material and not "teach." Even excellent teachers make the mistake of thinking that they have taught something but really have only covered something. Are you a teacher or are you a facilitator? Today, there are more and more schools offering on line courses to high school students. They have to in order to compete with private schools and meet the demands of parents who support it. This is good because it allows non-compulsory courses to be offered that would otherwise not be offered (like media and business courses and various English courses like writers craft or literature). The downside is, you guessed it, there is no teaching. When I was assigned my first two on-line courses and was trained in how to administer on line courses, I was told that I was not to stand at the front of the class and teach.

Whatever system you work in, make a conscious effort to put yourself in the mindset of your students. Brain researcher and differentiated instruction expert and author, Kathleen Nunley states: "...the vast majority of problems in classrooms are control issues. Shift the control, and the problems significantly decrease or disappear." At this point, I should point out that I am reluctant to agree with the word 'disappear' because I have never met a teacher who never had behavior problems. So if you want to expect all behavior problems to disappear, be mindful enough not to get discouraged when and if there are problems. It is akin to my telling myself that I'm not going to keep losing my cell phone or my keys all the time. Sooner or later, we all misplace something. When I say I never have met a teacher who has not had behavior problems, that is true but I have met some who claim that they never have behavior problems. Claiming and trying to project yourself as the best teacher in the school or oozing a "better than you" attitude has a whole litany of negative side effects in accordance to the law of attraction which we will get into, for now just simply note that it is for lack of a better term, "bad karma." The best teacher will sometimes have difficult students to deal with. Just as in life in general, the most positive people will have horrible things to deal with and go through. This is reality. Teachers are natural problem solvers and as such, are already in a good position to be awesome positive thinkers. Think about it. Nunley goes on to say: "Most of us in education know that students who are off task and disruptive are doing so for one of two reasons: either they are unable (or at least feel unable) to complete the task, or they are playing power games with the teacher in an attempt to maintain a sense of control. Both of these reasons are easy to eliminate." Essentially, you need to make students think and feel comfortable and make them think they are in control but always affirm that you are in control because you are. There are books written on the psychology of perception that show how easy our brains are tricked; we know this is true otherwise advertising would not be effective. So "advertise" your course. Your students will think they need to take your course and will feel good in your class. I recommend using the following affirmation: "I am free to differentiate my instruction so that there is more learning going on and the process is enjoyed by all."

CHAPTER 7

BE KIND IN THE CLASSROOM AND THE STAFF ROOM

Not all teaches are fair and thus not all teachers are kind. Do you have a reputation of someone who is kind? If you were to poll your co-workers or students would they agree with you? Being kind is all about being open-minded and fair. The alternative to this produces ineffective results.

At some point in our career, we overinflate a mark or grade too harshly. Affirm grading everything effectively. Affirm that you grade the success of the learning process, not the product (focusing on the objectives learned). Affirm that your students will seek out collegial support as they work toward mastery. Affirm that you will effectively watch for natural developmental interests and tie into these. If they do this you can use that lingo in your report card comments. It's actually easy.

Just when you think you have everything working in your classroom, you may find that the staff room is the last place you want to be. You will always have difficult people you will encounter in the workplace. Some of these people annoy you and others are your close friend most days but occasionally strike you as offensive. And you may even find yourself asking yourself, "how can this person be a teacher!?" In *The Amazing Results of Positive Thinking* by

Norman Vincent Peale, there is a chapter called "The Kind of People People Like." In essence, if you want to be liked and respected, get to accepting and liking all people. Therefore, these difficult people you encounter are probably not following this principle, moreover, if you are letting them get under your skin, neither are you! This knowledge represents a mitigating reason that should keep you from losing your patience or composure with such people. Peale states: "Look behind actions and see the real person. If you try to help him be his best self, you will win esteem and confidence. If, in trying situations, you show a deep understanding and patience for a person, not only he, but others also will like you very much indeed."

There may be a workplace where a transfer is the order of the day. There's no shame in this, so don't let your pride get in the way. Early in my career I was seriously contemplating leaving the profession due in large part to a horribly unsupportive administrator who was by all accounts a bully (who we will learn more about later). I put in for a transfer every year for five years (I was not practicing the use of affirmations at the time) and finally I requested a leave of absence at which point the superintendent granted me a transfer (to the school which I consider to be the best school I could ask to work for). I recall him saying, "change is good" in reference to my transfer. He knew. Looking back at those first five years, on one hand, I had more than enough union-log entries to file a grievance against Principal No-Support, though on the other hand, I could have been practicing affirmations and just as importantly, taking a genuine interest more often in people and always thinking of them as important. If you are connected with people it is because you are concerned for them, this tends to improve success and what do we know about success? It leads to happiness. Actually, happiness leads to success and additional success leads to all kinds of treats being attracted into our lives which results in more happiness, so there is a full cycle.

Think of relationships. What happens when we are not connected? It's an absolute. When I think back to the most dysfunctional relationship of my life (an experience which saw me access EAP goal-orientated therapy), I can a) forgive myself for the mistakes I made in terms of communication barriers, b) forgive the other person and wish them well, and c) laugh in solace knowing that I won't be in that situation again or if I am I will be better at handling it. Problems in relationships with friends, family members, loved ones, co-workers, students, parents and administrators, often start with what we perceive as criticism. Going back to relationships briefly, the number one cause of divorce is finances. Shouldn't it be adultery? Before I was married, I was cheated on in a previous relationship and know that when we get cheated on, we think it's a criticism. What are we not doing right that would lead this person to go out and find someone else? So we think we have to change and we stay in the relationship. What is known as the law of attraction causes an unpleasant side effect here. When we let criticism get to us, guess what happens? We are not fun to be around. Anyone can handle criticism. Thinking positive at all times takes care of this. As Peale says, "People who are able to turn criticism into a positive situation are going to attract friends."

When teachers go to the bar after work on a pay-day or Friday or whenever, what do they talk about? Is it positive or negative? Is it kind? For the most part, teachers complain about their students, their administrators, how the staff is more dysfunctional this year than last year, their students' parents; they complain about their students some more, and they argue about things because complaining about their students gets their mindset locked to what I would call collegial confrontation. They will argue about whether or not teaching is a vocation or if it is noble. They will generally argue whether or not it is a thankless job. They may discuss what careers are perhaps less noble than education. They may go on to talk about which jobs are apparently more important because after all, teachers don't "save lives"; but such teachers who think this way will in doing so, associate subconsciously and collectively, paramedics, surgeons, politicians, police, firefighters, (etc) with better livelihoods. This can be a negative affirmation on their own career depending on how they feel about work. Also, teachers, when in a group, will typically scrutinize other teachers that they deem as thinking and projecting that these other teachers are better teachers then everyone else. This is ironic, however, because in doing so, they themselves are doing just that. In reality not all teachers are equal. There are exemplary, excellent, good, satisfactory, and incompetent teachers. Think of an exemplary teacher for a minute... Now, can you honestly picture that teacher at a bar gossiping about co-workers and criticizing co-workers who give the impression they think they are better than everyone else. If you can, maybe they are not exemplary. Teachers who go around giving the impression they are perfect and they are loved by all are not quite exemplary for if they were, they wouldn't be going around carrying on the way they do. Such teachers may have issues inside and/or outside of school but why would you waste time being negative by complaining about them behind their back? Is it therapeutic for you to do so? If that is what you think maybe you should give the opposite a try. Teachers have a bad habit of being teacher-haters. They will sometimes blame teachers for issues that have more to do with administration just as they tend to blame administration for things that have more to do with a board's executive council or the government. Also, it's really particularly sad when teachers get together and pass judgment on department heads and program leaders which unfortunately they so often do. I've often heard the argument that program leaders are selfish and get what they want to teach, getting all grade twelve university level courses and how unfair it is that they find out teaching assignments before anyone else; and how if only they themselves were a head of a department, things would be different. This is low self-esteem thinking. As if department heads run the school! Well if you think that your department heads run the school, than that is your perception and that is the reality you are creating. As much as you don't want that reality you are choosing it. And ah yes, if only they were a department head they would be altruistic and volunteer to teach the most challenging classes to give the newer teachers a break. Of course in reality:

1) The only person who has a final say on classroom assignment is the boss, the principal

2) Department heads are just as disappointed or happy with their teaching assignments as anyone else and usually do have a mix of academic and applied classes, though no matter how much this happens the typical perception seems to stand.

3) If I was in a position where the principal said "Robert, you can pick whatever six classes you want to teach this year" as if that would ever happen, but we keep this crazy misconception alive and well, I would pick all grade twelve university level classes. Why wouldn't I? I'm not less of a teacher, I'm not less of a person, the grade twelve academic students aren't less deserving of good teachers than the applied students. I realize though you might jump at an opportunity to do what I just said I wouldn't for various self-less reasons and that is to be commended.

4) There's not only nothing immoral about doing what you specifically want to do but it's smart. You will have more energy and enthusiasm and you will be more goal-orientated and growth-orientated and insight-orientated

for it and subsequently, be more likely to be promoted to bigger and better opportunities that exceed your own initial expectations.

One of the worst things we can do as a teacher is become jealous of a co-worker. You don't have to be a union rep to know that some teachers hate on each other and are out to get each other. I have been jealous of co-workers and I realize now how nonsensical it really is. Rhonda Byrne put it quite eloquently in *The Power*: "If you meet someone who has qualities you wish you had, love those qualities and feel good about those qualities in that person, and you are bringing those qualities to yourself. If someone is smart, beautiful, or talented, love those qualities and you choose those things for *you!*"

So ask yourself, how do you feel when your co-worker lands the program leader or consultant position that you were going for? How would you feel if one of your co-workers inherited millions of dollars? What if you did an OK job chairing a sport team or extra-curricular club and the year that you stepped down someone else came along and there was much greater success under their leadership? How would you feel? What about when your co-worker gets a new car or house or wins a teacher of the year award? You ought to be excited for them in any of these cases, because as it turns out, if you are jealous of them you will deny yourself these positive experiences. I always tended to be most jealous when in June, classroom teaching assignments for the following year were announced and I never quite got my dream semester let alone my dream year and I would see other teachers getting all senior academic classes. If I feel jealous of other teachers' teaching schedules and dwell on how much I do not want the teaching assignment that I have been given, I am ensuring that I will never get the schedule I want. This is because of the law of attraction: "…when you say, 'No I don't want that,' you are saying *yes* to the law of attraction. When you say, 'the traffic is horrible,' 'The service is really bad,' 'They're always late,' 'It's too noisy in here,' 'That driver is a lunatic,' I've been on hold for so long,' you are saying *yes* to these things and you are including more of all of them in your life" (*The Power*).

CHAPTER 8

POSITIVE THINKING PLAIN AND SIMPLE V. FEAR

Positive thinking stimulates fresh and creative ideas. "To stimulate abundance, think. Really think there is a way to better conditions. And if you think it in your mind, you can think it into actuality" (Peale). If you are reading this thinking that's crazy, cheesy, too good to be true, too simple, and/or too naive, then you are right about one thing, it won't work for you. Unlike animals, humans can talk to themselves and listen to our own thoughts and this ability is there for a reason I would think. Have you ever caught yourself saying to yourself in your head "Good job!"? Of course you have, we all have. Clearly, we cherish moments in our lives that we perceive as lucky and we fear those that are not. And we think of ourselves as either lucky or unlucky and optimistic or pessimistic.

One of my favorite TV shows of all time was *Star Trek Voyager* which featured one of my all time favorite characters, Kathryn Janeway. There is one episode called "Thaw" where the crew of Voyager encounters a planet that has recently entered an ice age. They discover a series of stasis chambers where a small group of people are mentally connected to an artificial environment that turned horribly wrong. There is a clown who is the personification of fear and keeps people imprisoned and forces them to comply to his commands lest they be killed by their own thoughts. When some crew members become enslaved, Janeway outsmarts "Fear". She says, "I've known fear. It's a very healthy thing most of the time. You warn us of danger, remind us of our limits, protect us from carelessness. I've learned to trust fear. You know as well as I do that fear only exists for one purpose - to be conquered." With Fear's dying breath, he asks, "What will become of us — of me?" To which Janeway replies, "Like all fear, you eventually... vanish." Fear then says, "I'm afraid", Janway whispers.... "I know..." Fear whispers, "Drat!" and disappears. I once had a co-worker tell me he once overcame his fear of heights by bungee jumping and likewise had a fear of snakes and put a large snake around his neck to overcome that fear. He said he could never stand to have something like a fear over him. I have a fear of sharks but I have no plans to go swimming in the deep ocean. But some fears don't have to be overcome. Others do. All can. What does this have to do with teaching you ask? Because teachers can fear change, stress and challenge. To be sure, fear is something all teachers experience. Many teachers have a fear of the first day of class. Some fear parent teacher night. Others still, teacher performance appraisals. Fear is a powerful force. It can be an affliction. Some teachers fear the uneasy anxiety of getting behind. Sometimes we feel scared but know not what it is we fear and therefore feel helpless to fight back against it. As in all aspects of life, fear sometimes can be not something to be pinpointed but a whole litany of things and thus, a fight seems futile. But like any good Starfleet Captain, we should not believe in the existence of a no-win situation otherwise fear can be a cloud that hovers over us in which case it will bring with it bad luck. Fear gets in the way of happiness. Therefore, fear affects our ability to think and communicate. It can even affect health since it is a form of stress.

Today, many teachers are on anti-depressants and/or medication for high blood pressure or cholesterol. Surly, they must be dealing with stress and fear factors in their lives. I recall one day at school that was particularly stressful and everything that could go wrong was going wrong as if Murphy's Law was an exact science that day and I had severe chest pains and thought I was perhaps going to have a heart-attack. It was first period and I knew it was by far one of the most challenging classes I had ever taught and I remember thinking, "Oh this is great, if I lose consciousness in cardiac arrest, these students can't be relied on to respond appropriately and I'll die." It obviously wasn't really a heart-attack because if it was, my negative thoughts at the time surly would have worsened the attack. In theory, in a medical emergency like an actual heart-attack, perhaps the victim experiences fear and that fear speeds up the crisis. I've also had times in the classroom where my left eyelid exhibited violent palpitation twitching that I can't begin to describe to you how annoying it was. I remember Googleing the symptom and the treatment/prevention was listed as more sleep, less caffeine, less stress, and less fear. This translated into "no immediate treatment possible!" Although for the record, Visene seems to help, perhaps due to a placebo effect. It is important to do something about fear. It may be impossible to stop an eye from twitching on command but it is never impossible to let go of fear and stress. You have to attract little strategies into your life that counter these. Ever since my first year as a teacher, I use a stress ball and carry it with me most of the time and I find it soothing.

We can't become the type of teacher we consciously or subconsciously fear of becoming. We need to exorcise our fears but first we need to exorcise our demons which include meanness, hate, resentment, and jealousy. These are the culprits of a toxic working environment. With fear, thoughts which come when we don't expect them, the Janeway frontal attack method is not always ideal so much as the displacement and substitution method of eliminating it.

So, avoid fear!

What else do teachers fear?

-false accusations

-vindictive students

-stress in general

-class assignments

-bad administrators

-a genuine fear that to relinquish any control at all to the students would ultimately lead to chaos

-tension

And last, but not least, parents. We love supportive parents who back us up and we dread the teacher-hating parent who sees that their son or daughter can do no wrong. Mindfulness in parent communication can make our job much easier. I have, for example learned that when a parent is blaming you for something, you can have go-to statements like, " I understand that this is an emotional situation." "It's natural to advocate for your child." "We are all looking for success." "I hear you."

Don't say negative affirmations to parents, some are obvious like "Your son/daugher's behavior is unacceptable" is too negative but did you know that you should not say "I totally get where you're coming from"? It's construed as committal. The most negative people we will ever encounter in our careers our parents who are negative people, some of whom have mental health disorders and we have to be patient with them. Some of them are simply blind to their son/daughter's behavior; I have said many times that it's so difficult to be patient with the feeble-minded but we must love them and smile sweetly at their self-deluded ways.

The fact is that positive thinking works and just because it doesn't always work is not validation for abandoning it, since the alternative can only equal a life with more stress. I once read something that Dr. David R. Hamilton wrote about positive thinking in general and I thought it would be worth a try to apply to a school setting: "I have noticed that I can sometimes effortlessly change the atmosphere in a room simply by thinking how much I appreciate each person there and then feeling the appreciation. Quite often there's a profound transformation right before my eyes. A cold or even openly hostile environment can be transformed into a warm, loving, happy, peaceful, or forgiving one."

CHAPTER 9

NEVER HATE A COMPUTER

I am going to use a computer as a metaphor for the education system in general and I will get to that but first, know that at some point in my career, I got type-casted as the number- one complainer of computer problems at my school. And as any teacher at my school will tell you, our computers more often than not perform poorly, but there are some teachers who literally never complain about this reality. So it makes it less of a reality for those teachers. Teachers get frustrated when the photo-copier doesn't work (I myself am amazed how often the photo-copier jams, though I have recently found that when it jams, I think to myself that today I will save paper and do something else instead or if applicable, read the handout material to the class), or use the LCD, or the computers (etc). The photo-copier once jammed the morning before a teacher-appraisal observation visit from my principal! The stress! But I still was able to deliver a wonderful lesson. And believe me, I have horror stories about computer technical problems that have plagued my school to the point where it impeded on my lessons, too many to make reference to. And boards and schools do need to take their IT more seriously. In fact, it should be in the collective agreements that schools ensure computers work properly. This is one example of logistics. Logistics is an issue we ourselves can work on improving through affirmations. We will always have to deal with physical limitations, liability concerns, class size etc. When it comes to logistics, remember that the larger the problem is, the more creative the solution ought to be. In any event, complaining can block our creative process. I for one have learned this the hard way. Louise Hay has taught us that any computer problems we have our traced back to our thoughts! I bet that sounds odd to you. Yet, it is true. Cars are a better example. If you say "I hate my car" it's an easy negative affirmation to manifest again, (here I speak from experience) and even if you get a new car you will soon hate it because that is what you are affirming, according to Louise Hay. Remember, it does not make sense to hate something or someone because it is a waste of energy and it is always a negative affirmation and when it comes to objects, it makes even less sense because to hate is to take something personally, how can a car, a computer, or a photo-copier be out to get us? We are fooling ourselves at the delight of our pain body when we do this. It is a trap. Do not fall for it. Notice yourself reacting in a positive way to technical difficulties and then be grateful that you are mindful enough to stay in control but do not anticipate technical difficulties. Otherwise, you might end up like some of the characters on the *Seinfeld* episode where George, Krammar, Mr. Frank Costanza, and Llyod Braun use the mantra: "serenity now." They don't do it right and it backfires. Frank, for example is advised to say "serenity now" aloud every time his blood pressure is in danger of going up, but he yells it instead. George hatches a scheme to sell more computers: to buy them himself and return them later for a refund; however, continual use of the phrase "serenity now" has an adverse effect on his sales. George stores computers in Kramer's apartment. Kramer has a nervous breakdown and breaks the computers. George's father blames him for nearly bankrupting his company. George then tells his dad to instead say "hoochie-mama" in place of "serenity now", which his father follows. This episode's plot was inspired by real-life events in the life of writer Steve Koren. While driving with his arguing parents, Koren was bewildered to hear his father shout "Serenity now!" at the top of his lungs as part of a rage controlling exercise and questioned whether or not the phrase was meant to be screamed. Probably not.

Now, I said that the computer was a metaphor of the education system in general. Just as it is counter-productive to hate the computer that never works or the photo-copier for that matter, it is useless to hate on the education system itself. Would you want a police officer, lawyer, or judge to hate the justice system? No and yet there are some out there. We do not make the best teachers if we hate the system. The other extreme would be to love the system and never seek change. Think of your country. Do you love it? Some people that live in this country hate it and in doing so are not part of any solutions. Some love it blindly and therefore can't be a part of any solution either. Nationalism can and does get in the way of healthy skepticism. Not enough of us are mindful of this or voter turnouts would be higher.

I was listening to Richard Syrett on his talk show once where he spoke with a free-lance investigative reporter about the decline of public education and the absence of any meaningful instruction in critical thinking and logic. Once upon a time, Jon Rappoport says, there were textbooks which listed fifteen or twenty traditional logical fallacies, and students were taught how to spot those fallacies in any argument or presentation. In most schools, the subject of logic has been lost. Therefore, the ability to analyze written and spoken material has faded into obscurity. I would add to this that if we were teaching mindfulness in the first place, logic would be taught and learned naturally. If the focus is not mindfulness but logic itself, then it will fall under the context of literacy and thus only the students in academic-level English classes will truly benefit from it! Besides, teaching logic does not address the issue of parents who do not trust the judgment of teachers. Often at parent teacher interviews, parents question teacher's marks. I knew a teacher once that turned his mark book to a parent and said, "Write down whatever mark you want your kid to have. I'll give him 100% if you want because it's meaningless if you don't trust my judgment."

Has public education descended into a stagnant pool of political correctness, fraudulent graduation rates, and "new values?" Has logic been diluted and discarded to a point of no return? Hopefully, if you are in this profession, you do not believe so. Hopefully, you believe with all that you are, that the education system will improve. Such improvement depends on your thinking just that.

We have an obligation as teachers to enable students to take apart a written text, an argument, a visual presentation—and discover whether it is valid, whether it truly makes sense, whether it has holes in it. Otherwise, the education system is incapable of improving because we will have a future generation of parents who are not supportive of such change.

CHAPTER 10

PERSPECTIVE COMES THE WAY IT ALWAYS DOES

Our brains and minds are fascinating things. I think there are forces at work which we can not comprehend. I read an article once: "X-Files 'hum' phenomenon could be over-sensitive hearing- Scientists have dismissed claims that people are being severely effected by a low-level hum - as featured in *The X-Files* - saying it is the effect of over-sensitive hearing." "If you're sitting by a table waiting for exam results and the phone rings you jump out of your skin. Waiting for a teenager to come home from a party - the key in the door sounds really loud. Your internal gain is sensitized." According to Dr Baguley, the problem comes when an individual fixes on a possibly innocuous background sound, and this act of concentration then triggers the body's "internal gain", boosting the volume. "It becomes a vicious cycle," he explains. "The more people focus on the noise, the more anxious and fearful they get, the more the body responds by amplifying the sound, and that causes even more upset and distress." ...

To make a long story short, we are constantly being affected by the sounds, images, and feelings around us but I think we only notice on a conscious level one of the three in particular depending on if we are auditory, visual, or tactile people. Speaking of X-Files, I have always had an interest in parapsychology and I have been known to listen to *Coast to Coast AM*, *The X Zone* and *The Richard Syrett Show* (paranormal radio talk shows). Maybe there is an alternate reality out there maybe several that are home to a much more fair life than this one, but as Clint Eastwood's character, William Money says in *Unforgiven*, "Deserve's got nothing to do with it." This universe brings difficulties to one and all and lots of them. Any one of which, can become a breaking point or a turning point depending on your perspective.

It all depends on how you take hold of any given situation. Will it help you in the long run or keep holding you down? "Mishaps are like knives, that either serve us or cut us, as we grasp them by the blade or the handle" so says author James Russell. Life has to have difficulties plain and simple. Imagine yourself on the last Friday of the year at school first thing in the morning before your first cup of coffee or tea and you are extremely drained and tired and now imagine yourself after a large double-double at Tim Horton's (or for my American readers, a grande latte at Starbucks). Perspective can make all the difference.

Norman Vincent Peale says: "A chief reason that people are beaten down by difficulty is simply that they allow themselves to think they can be beaten."

Always remember, you are indeed greater than any difficulty. By growing you can overcome your difficulties.

Other affirmations to now consider:

I am proud to be a teacher.

Teaching is one of the most honorable and noble of all professions.

I love what I do and know that my enthusiasm is contagious.

I bring knowledge, dedication, and understanding to my classroom.

I make a positive difference in my students' lives.

My students will be better people because of me, and I will be a better person because of them.

I know what I give to my students will come back to me in many wonderful and unexpected ways.

I dwell on my progress and learn from my mistakes.

I see good in all my students.

I know all is well in my classroom.

Do not be discouraged by a set back or your affirmations will be delayed. You have to let your affirmations go for them to work and not worry about how they are going to come into fruition.

Avoiding contact with parents is not a very competent habit to get into. Though it is so perfectly understandable why a teacher hates calling a parent when so many parents get aggressive and blame the teacher when confronted with their child's misbehavior.

A sadder reality in teaching is the accusations that are based on fact but there are also many false accusations that have ruined the career of innocent teachers. Teachers have often experienced a student running up to them and hugging them on the last day or at graduation and they either don't hug back and feel guilty and awkward or they do hug back out of reflex and then feel paranoid. Vindictive students can make false accusations, vandalize, steal, threaten, and physically assault teachers. This has led to much stress in the teaching profession. Stress in general is worrisome. Heart disease runs in my family and I catch myself sometimes thinking that the stress of my line of work will increase the chances that I will succumb to a heart-attack or stroke of some sort but then I remind myself that a) I am me, not my relatives and b) when your number is up, your number is up (i.e., do not worry!). Class assignments can be a form of stress or resentment or discouragement as we all know as well. Rarely does a teacher get an assignment and say, "YES! This is exactly what I wanted! Perfect! I even have the ideal class list(s)!" Bad principals do exist. Deal with it. As I have found, the great thing about having an unsupportive principal is that when you do have a very supportive and positive one you will all the more appreciate that person in your life. If a school has a toxic working environment it is ultimately the principal who is responsible. A genuine fear that to relinquish any control at all to the students would ultimately lead to chaos is common. Is the root cause of your fear that you are not assertive enough with students? If so the solution is a simple matter of affirmations. As for tension, it can simply be attacked at the point of conversation and talk. You know that you can talk yourself into being tense. A verbal statement is an articulated thought. We can learn to counter this once and for all by using quiet, composed tones and words. Elevating the voice is more often than not counter-productive. Remember, positive thinking is stronger than negative thinking since faith trumps fear, so fear not.

Some teachers have been blessed with a powerful or authoritative presence. However, some teachers spend so much time on control that it becomes their biggest source of pride. Control is important. Learning is more important. You need to affirm for yourself a vision. Brain researcher Dr. Katherine Nunley simply puts it well: "For a teacher, that vision is an idea of what skills or knowledge you need your students to have. Get an idea of the goals of your curriculum and your personal standards of student excellence. Envision a successful classroom." Envisioning is what I am getting at. Affirmations lead you on a path to visualize new realities. As politics shows us clearly in any country's history, and as James Kouzes and Barry Posner have written, "There's nothing more demoralizing than a leader who can't clearly articulate why we're doing what we're doing."

If your students are to respect you they need to know from you why they are learning what they are learning. Affirm that you are doing this. Affirm that you are an exemplary teacher and also affirm that you are more than a teacher. You are a facilitator, instructor, coach, and leader.

Affirm that your students are learning self-control and responsibility because punishment alone does little to accomplish this. However, be weary that punishments will always be necessary as it can temporarily stop misbehavior and more importantly, it deters other students.

Affirm your communication skills are ideal. These can be used to assist students who are themselves experiencing problems. For further information on this, read the chapter on communication skills in *Classroom Management for Secondary Teachers* by Edmund T. Emmerm Carolyn M.

Evertson, Barbara S. Clements, and Murry E. Worsham. This book delves into the importance of the concepts of constructive assertiveness, empathic responding, and problem solving.

Affirm that your eye contact, body language, messages, voice features, and facial features are assertive and never unassertive or hostile.

Affirm that you always respond as a patient attentive listener when students ask the age-old rhetorical questions/statements that annoy so many teachers:

-Is this on the test?

-why do we have to do this?

-this is stupid!

-School sucks!

-I can't understand this!

-Why do you hate me?

-Do I have to sit here? I'm not sitting here.

-We don't care!

Same goes for parents you deal with:

-Quit picking on my son/daughter.

-I'm a man's man, we didn't have to learn Shakespeare when I was in school.

-An open mind is an empty mind!

-My child is upset and needs more help. She says she doesn't understand anything.

Same goes for co-workers:

-Really, you were having problems with Johnny? He's always a perfect angel in my class!

-That third period is going to drive me up the wall. They've been impossible lately!

Same goes for administrators:

-What do you mean a fight broke out in your class? How could that happen!?

The single worst experience of my career was the four years I worked under a bully administrator. I will share with you some of the details and explain what I could have done differently and you will no doubt infer what the principal could have done differently.

She used to give all teachers a mark on their report cards. This in and of itself was unprofessional (treating us like students and pitting the staff against each other and her constant negative bashing of my report card marks and comments was outlandish). In retrospect, this was insignificant. I should not have taken it so personally nor should I have complained so much about it. Thankfully, most principals do not do this and it's something to be gracious of. She always gave me less than twenty-four hours notice (and sometimes less than one hour's notice) of parent meetings and IPRC meetings. I can see that this was a reflection of her lack of organizational skills but I too at the time had poor organizational skills and therefore this is more a case of my hating something in someone else that I hate about myself. Again, most principals do not do this but when they do the better perspective would be something like: "this does not always happen this way and sometimes we have to be mindful of parents schedules not just our own and IPRC meetings are important and as a good teacher I can speak to a parent about their son or daughter confidently with or without notice." There was a behavior-problem student in grade six who came up to me once when I was teaching grade seven and said, "I'm going to be in your class starting Monday." So, the principal here never told me. But the student was nice enough to. Of course I took that very personally at the time but looking back, it was probably done because the principal knew

I would get my back up. This principal used to dismissed students to an unsupervised yard. Instead of complaining about it, I should have politely brought the issue to her attention. She would scold me in front of staff and students sometimes. This was very wrong of her to do but given the negative affirmations I was giving out at that point in my life I can't be surprised that I was attracting that kind of experience into my life. She would often say, "Did you tell him/her why you sent them to the office?" And when I said "No" She would smile as if relieved that now she didn't have to deal with it. Again, not professional on her part but clearly, if I was mindful I would never send a student out of a class without clearly telling them why no matter how obvious it is to me or other students in the class. When a student asks why they are being sent out to of the class, remember that the student was being mindful in the first place and is probably 100% honest in asking because they actually do not know the reason why they are being removed. The principal refused to suspend students for fighting. I do not understand why this was so but I do know principals everywhere are usually reluctant to suspend and we as teachers should not be considered with whether or not someone is suspended if we ourselves do not have the authority to suspend. We have the right to remove a student from a classroom and the right to suggest a suspension and beyond that, we have to put our trust in the administration.

Then, there were ALP meetings where the principal would only go over negative critiques of it. I am glad that happened because although I took it personally at the time and did not agree with the flack, it probably was a factor in my being so determined to be a better teacher and it totally made me more appreciative of subsequent principals and vice principals who would have more tact when giving constructive feedback and praise.

When I think back to those meetings and her telling me to do things I was already doing like standing at the front door of the class and greeting students daily, I believe this was less a case of her being out to chase me out of the profession (which is how I felt at the time) to a matter of her not being mindful to notice all the work that I was doing.

I would apply for a transfer every year and she would tell me that I wasn't going to get one. I bought into that and it became a reality. I could feel myself giving up.

She would always give me report card corrections back three days after everyone else. If I was more mindful at the time, I would have put more time and effort into the report cards and there would not have been so many corrections to be made. So, I take full responsibility on this issue, moreover, I believe report cards have gone from being one of weaknesses to one of my strengths and this is directly linked to this past experience. A bad experience can be a great learning experience. She told me I could teach Grade eight if, the grade eight teacher got a transfer. When he did indeed get one, she posted the job and conducted job interviews. I got the job anyway. Maybe it was wrong of me to take that move personally and maybe she was directed by the board/human resources to have interviews. Her teacher performance appraisals were full of false statements and she classified me as "satisfactory." I think this was what I detested the most but guess what? When I got my next appraisal by a different principal five years later, it exceeded my hopes and expectations as a reflection of my specific affirmations. She made me teach math when it wasn't necessary and math is my worst subject which is a disservice to students by any perspective. However, I should have thought and said, "This is a challenge that I am up for because it will lead to my own math skills improving."

She never in any way shape or form complimented me. For all I know though, maybe she did compliment me behind my back and I just didn't know it. She allowed me no creative control over planning the grade eight trip. It was literally her way or the highway. But I must admit I was not assertive at all when it came to this. She told me my class was more challenging than the grade seven class but she told the grade seven teacher that her grade sevens would be the most challenging group of her career. Look, sometimes people are just plain wrong, it does not mean they are liars. When several boys were caught giving Ex-lax to younger students, she did nothing. This is an example of something she did that I can't justify but that's OK, I bring it up as well because if someone has done something that is wrong from all angles, you can still resist getting upset when you consider that a) in doing so you are committing a negative affirmation on your own accord and b) karma may come back and cause distress in that person's life and if that's the case, the person in question may be entitled to sympathy as opposed to feelings of ill-will. She allowed a student to be in the computer lab unsupervised who had been previously caught surfing pornography. This is just a reflection of her not being mindful and me taking something personal at the time that had nothing to do with me. A student threatened to bring a gun to school.

Nothing was done. I hope that this was a case where something was done but the teachers were just never made aware of it. She would supervise other teachers' students at lunch or recess who had overdue work but not mine. But those teachers were probably more assertive in implying their need for support than I was. And she would tell me that I had to supervise my students and not let them out for recess or lunch if they had overdue work. Well, a) that was just a case of my not knowing my rights to not be subject to an extra workload and b) it was actually good advice in theory. When there was a lock-down at the school and the police had to come she did nothing to follow up on it, no staff meeting no debrief, no memo, just a total ignore the problem and it will go away attitude. She said publicly that at this school they put their best teachers in grade one; I look back on that and realize she was just not mindful enough to realize that such a statement was offensive to non-grade one teachers.

One student in particular was extremely volatile and constantly harassed females in the class and whenever he would to the point of being sent to the office, she would send him back even if it was multiple trips to the office in one day. Wrong of her? Absolutely. Was I doing enough on my end? Absolutely not. Anytime I would take a sick day or a personal day she would ask me about it. Nobody else on staff was ever approached in this way. Many of whom had more sick days than I. Maybe she honestly did not know that she was violating the collective agreement at the time. When I had a supply teacher, and the supply teacher would send a student to the office, she would be heard saying "Well, Rob's not here so we can just send him/her back to class." I now know how much energy can be drained by concerning yourself with things that happen when you are not at the school. She would stand in the hall and watch students line up at the water fountain after phys.ed and not say a word to them but would sternly tell me, "Better tell them to hurry along." I think I did handle that correctly by ignoring it and not letting it bother me too much. She would not allow me to write "Keep it up" or "Keep up the good work" on my report cards. I hated that but maybe she honestly was under direct direction to implement and enforce this anal retentive policy. If anything I should not have let it bug me so much since it is not a personal attack.

I have a whole union log notebook filled with many other examples all of which are equally anal retentive or sad. At the end of that fourth year I put in for a transfer and did not get it. So, I put in for a leave of absence for a year off. That same day however, I was offered a transfer to a high school. The following year was the greatest year of my professional life. If only my personal life would have been positive to go along with it, it would have been the greatest year of my life. And that year, several e-mails from former co-workers from the previous school found their way to my inbox telling me how "bleak" things had become at that old school. The principal in question retired. Now I know that there are lots of things she could have done differently and that she was at times incompetent as a principal, presumably incompetent at times as a teacher before that. But what could I have done differently? I mentioned some specific things already but there are three main general things:

1) I could have been more patient, more positive, and communicated with her on a social level. That would have improved things.

2) I could have filed a grievance (there is a time and place for grievances which we will get into). It would have improved things because I'm sure it would have resulted in an apology and a transfer for one or both of us. Since then I have seen teachers file grievances for far less and win. This tells me I should have, could have, would have but it also shows me that some teachers have forgotten that teaching is a vocation and don't realize how worse off they could be.

3) Most effectively, I could have resigned in lieu of not being granted a transfer. It makes no sense to stay in a job that is clearly a toxic working environment. It takes no time finding work as a substitute teacher or part time college instructor and about fifteen weeks to find full time work as a teacher, if you are willing to relocate. In such a case you may need to resign to save your physical and mental health. Inconvenient though it is, any jobless person can use the law of attraction to get a new job that they enjoy. However, had I had initiated any or all of these, I might not have gotten the subsequent job at the other school which I loved so much (had I have opted for option 1, I would have toughed it out for another year, she would have retired and I would probably still be there, had I have opted for 2, I may have been transferred to a school I don't want to be at because of its assignment for me or because of its location, or had I had opted for option 3, I might not even have stayed in the profession and you wouldn't be reading this book. I must, therefore, believe that "blessings in disguise" do exist. By the way, when logging bullying behavior by an administrator, or co-worker which

you should, be mindful that it is possible to be unaware of your own issues. If you are the only one perceiving the alleged bullying, it becomes very hard to act on. For the record, in my case, the thought, "is it just me?" crossed my mind but several co-workers often assured me I was being treated unfairly. In fact, that principal's favorite teacher on staff once told me "You could tell her the world is round and she would correct you."

You know deep down inside if you need to forgive someone. I have forgiven this principal many times over. There is power in forgiveness. There are times when we need to forgive an administrator, parent, family member, friend, ourselves, student, or co-worker. As a teacher, it should be easy to forgive a student. For me, out of all the people I have ever had to forgive, this principal was the single hardest one. It took the longest by far. And now I wish her well. I even realize that my dislike of her was in part rooted at the time to things I did not like about myself. Self-hatred thoughts are just thoughts and a thought can be changed. A thought can be changed. A thought can be changed. A thought can be changed. Do you see the affirmation there?

All principals pick and chose when they ignore a student's behavior. Sometimes, they ignore a behavior because they feel that it is the teacher's responsibility to handle the student in question. I have to own-up to times when I have not dealt effectively enough with my own students.

Like Louise Hay, I believe that humans are good and they try there best at any given time. But I think that there is that less than one percent of the population (probably, more like less than 1/3rd of the population) that accounts for Hitler, Stallin, Ghangas Khan, Jack the Ripper, Osama Bin Ladden (etc) that are always going to choose to do bad, not including those who are sociopaths and psychopaths. Schools have these students before they are adults and it's when principals ignore these students that bullying, racism, and criminal behavior can get reinforced. There's not much a teacher can do in these cases but the more affirmations you use the less you will attract behavior problems to encounter (then you can enjoy less stress and less energy drainage).

So as you can see, perspective comes. But through affirmations it can come sooner than later.

CHAPTER II

YOU CAN'T PUNISH STUDENTS INTO THE VORTEX

You can't punish behavior-problem students and expect them to all of a sudden forget that they are behavior-problem students. If someone gets a speeding ticket, have they learned their lesson? Perhaps, at least temporarily, but they probably will speed again. And if you are fostering negative affirmations when you speed you are more likely to do so at the right time and the right place for police to catch you. There is a state of being that the teachings of Abraham refer to as a "harmonious vortex" where we are virtually impervious to bad luck and stress as we know it when in it. A little piece of Heaven right here on this planet. But it is not Heaven since it is impossible to live your entire life inside the vortex. I know this is a bummer. It's no wonder why so many people say "life is unfair." It can certainly seem that way. I certainly used to say it all the time and considered it an absolute. However, the good news is that when you are outside of the vortex there can be expansion by learning. When we have a student in our class who has a great deal of unfortunate circumstances going on in their life outside the school causing them to be non-compliant, we must not forget that we can't punish them into the "vortex." If we could punish people into this state of being then we would have eliminated crime by now by punishing criminals. I'm by no means an anarchist because there is a need for disciplinary measures in our schools and our society. But those have more to with protecting people. Take suspensions for example. Suspensions discipline students but more importantly they protect the other students in the class or the school.

In *Classroom Management For Secondary Teachers* by Edmund T. Emmer (and Carolyn M. Evertson, Barbara S. Clements, and Murray E. Worsham), there is a valuable chapter called "Choosing Rules and Procedures" in which student participation in rule setting is addressed. Consider the rules suggested and consider making these daily affirmations i.e. "my students will.... are.... always... bringing all needed material to class, seated and ready to work when the bell rings, respecting and being polite to all people, listening and staying seated when someone is talking, respecting other people's property, and obeying all school rules." And so on. Sooner or later, no matter how good a teacher you are, rules will be violated. I think of my best behaved class I have ever had and there were still some rule violations. Thankfully, more of the classes I have taught resemble that class and not the ENG3C "class from Hell" that caused me stress, heartburn, and headaches, but then again, ENG3C was a valuable learning experience. It is important for me to be gracious on both accounts.

Whenever rules are broken and they will be broken, we all know that you have the power to make things worse or make things better. It's the old proactive v. reactive. We can increase our ability to have positive feel-good results when rules are violated by affirming how these opportunities of conflict-resolution unfold. One type of consequence is usually prescribed by school policy, such as 'lates' and dress code violations but ultimately, the teachers enforce these. Don't be one of those teachers who tend to be lax with these rules. How will the students take your rules seriously if they know that you don't take the school rules seriously? So, affirm accordingly. And know and accept that students will always say, "But Mr. or Mrs. So and So always lets us listen to our I-Pods". Affirm that you plan consequences (but be careful that this does not become a negative affirmation). For example, "I deal with negative behavior effectively" is magnetically attracting negative behavior. Try, "I am mindful enough at all times to plan consequences with positive results ahead of time and this helps me use them consistently." Now you will be better able to communicate with students.

When I think back to ENG3C, I think of how loud the class was. It didn't matter if I was teaching or if there was a film or if there was a test, it was loud. 99% of classroom problems stem from noise level. Ideally, you need your class to be silent. This is dependent upon a quiet learning environment on the first day of class. So in theory, you never have to be more firm then on the first day of class. Group work is essential in any course during which time it is necessary to allow talking. Impress students with the importance of keeping talk focused on task. The noise level won't get too loud or uncomfortable if the students are talking about school work. Why would it? Affirm: "During the activity, I monitor the groups carefully and stop inappropriate behavior quickly at the individual or group level before it spreads to the whole class." Affirm: "I identify signals I can use to warn the class if the noise level gets too high." There is a great write- up and check-list on behavior management at http://www.unco.edu/teach/crm.html by the University of Coloroado. One thing I have always done and found that is effective is when I yell "YO!" when I need to re-gain the attention of the class. They all know to simultaneously yell back "YO!" followed by complete silence; literally, you can only hear the buzz of the lights. Of course this won't work with every group, and is only appropriate for grades 7-12, and will not work with all teachers. Affirm that you always find what works.

Keep a positive perspective and avoid over-dwelling on student misbehavior or inadequacies. All teachers should know how easy it is to get into a routine of seeing only faults and problems and overlooking the better features of students' behavior. We tend to complain about one student out of twenty-nine students. If you can't break this habit maybe you should consider a panel change (i.e. primary, junior, intermediate, senior, post-secondary). If you want your students to look forward to your class, and you do want that, you need to praise your students and focus on the positive and not spend your staff room time complaining about certain "usual suspects" students. Students expect to learn more than we tend to give them credit for. If your class was to fill out a survey on how supported they feel by you and they were honest, how would that turn out? Affirm that you communicate positive expectations to students, praise good performance, and, make your students feel that learning in your class is worth it (rewards for example is a good strategy). More students will attempt new tasks and reach goals if this is happening. The more this is happening in schools, the more we will see societal improvement which, let us not forget, is one of the purposes of the education system. Praise your students and remember to phrase your praise carefully. Simply saying "Good effort" is nothing new and does not comment on the academic accomplishment and is therefore not always effective. I can see why some principals don't allow that as a report card comment.

Bullies and racists who insist on projecting their hate to those around them flourish in many systems that border on being bully-friendly like in some states where governors don't consider bullying to be bullying when a student is bullied for their sexual orientation or in some various schools where bullies are often ignored by administrators. This is unfortunate. I like many teachers, have contemplated leaving the profession because of this. However, we as teachers can lower bullying despite the system. When I said that we can't punish students into the vortex where we want them, we need to keep in mind that we need to be in the vortex ourselves to expect our students to be there with us and secondly, this does not mean that students should be exempt from punishment. It just means that punishment alone can never be the solution. Bullying and racism should be dealt with. We should encourage each other to set goals to become principals so that we can infiltrate the system and deal with bullies and racists. I sometimes jokingly think that when a teacher becomes a vice principal they are shipped off to a dark room in Langley, Virginia and strapped in front of monitors where they are brainwashed to ignore behavior problems. Administrators and so-called "principal want-to-be's" tend to be anti-suspension and will say that if you suspend a student it rewards bad behavior and these suspended studednts go hang out at the mall all day. This is outrageous. Think about it. Rewarding bad behavior is when you ignore bad behavior and allow the bad behavior to be habitual. I don't know any student that gets suspended and goes to the mall and hangs out there all day by themselves while their friends are at school. If you are reading this and you understand why suspensions are a bad thing, e-mail me and explain it to me. After all, if I am to practice what I preach, then I am open to other points of view. It's most bizarre when schools claim to use a progressive discipline policy and in actual fact there is a reverse progression discipline in place. I've taught students that bullied and harassed students and made racist comments weekly and went from being suspended to being assigned detentions, to no noticeable consequence(s) at all.

As I implied in the previous perspective chapter, there is nothing more discouraging then when you have no support from administration. I had a student once who was coming to class every day refusing to do any work. During one class in particular, the class was writing a test and the student crumpled his up and threw it out and when the VP came by on his daily pop-in, I told him and his exact word response: "Easy for you to mark" and walked away. There was the time I gave a student a detention for throwing a ball in class for most of the class and refusing to hand it over. He then refused to attend the detention. He told the VP that he wasn't the one throwing the ball and would not serve the detention. The VP told him he would therefore have a suspended sentence for two weeks if he was issued a detention he would have to serve two. The student told the VP that if that happened he would only serve a single detention but that there was no way he would serve two, and walked away. The VP then looked at me smiled and said, "I think I just bought you two weeks." Discouraging? Yes? But then again, he's not the "principal from Hell" (if he is supportive more often than not, then that needs to be my focus). It can always be worse and it can always be better and it's up to us and only us if things get better or worse or stay the same tomorrow and the day after that and the week after that and the month after that and so on. I have respect for that vice principal, real respect; I have to be mindful of that respect. He respected me as well and I have to be mindful of that. Do I log the event? Yes. Logs can be used when you feel in your professional opinion that you need to have a student removed from your class. Or they can come in handy for a parent meeting. Be careful with logs though. There are two extremes. No logs at all are an affirmation of ignorance or laziness. Too many logs can be an affirmation that you want misbehavior so that you have something to log or an affirmation that you want to mount a case against a particular student. No matter how unlikable a student is, your preference should be to see the student mature and succeed and learn. That is a powerful affirmation. Say it a loud now: "No matter how unlikable a student is, my preference is for the student to mature, succeed, and learn." This particular affirmation could have come in handy several years ago. I had a male student who I taught in junior high. At the beginning, I had an excellent rapport with him. Over the next two years, his behavior regressed dramatically. By the time he was in grade eight, he misbehaved daily without question. He was the most infamous bully in the school. I would have taken a pay-cut if it meant not having him in my classroom. He was one of those rare students that has a combination of factors that lead to exceptional circumstances of behavior. But years later, I would come across his first day of school information getting to know you sheet he filled out on his first day of school in grade seven. He said: "I like the summer and jumping on my trampoline. I love pizza, it's the best food ever. My favorite song is 7 *Nation Army* by the White

Stripes and my favorite cartoon is Spongbob Square Pants. It has dawned on me that these "411" sheets we make and have students fill out on the first day should be used as affirmations. When they fill them out, what they write is usually quite honest and positive. Even the occasional rebellious student that uses it to spew out harsh sarcasm, you will find their innocence shining through. So keep them in your classroom or room at home and go through them as you do affirmations and if you pray you can use them during prayer too to pray over and bless them. You will find yourself more sympathetic to them and in turn, you will have less problems with them and a much better rapport with them.

Remember, you can't punish the student into the vortex. This is a misconception formed deep in the recesses of our pain body where we tell ourselves "I'll tear a strip out of him or her tomorrow and that will be that."

When I think back to Teacher's College, we clearly we're never taught this directly. The term affirmation-based pedagogy was not known. But indirectly, the data was there for us. I had fun digging out my old notebook from teachers' college that smelled of my parent's basement. First page: "Socratic Method." It seems to me that affirmations can go hand in hand with getting students to realize that there is great value in the effort of thinking on your own, this is why we as student teachers were taught to encourage students to develop understanding as well as absorbing facts. Socrates knew about the power of positive and negative-based thought. He said that argument alone does not lead to knowledge.

Let's continue on this return to teachers' college. In the course "Philosophy and Education" after Socrates, we learned about Locke, Rousseau, Pestazzoli, Froebel, Montessori, and Piaget, Sartre, Camus, Nietzshe, Kierkegard, Pascal, and Dewey. I did not become a fan of Rousseau till I watched *Lost* and appreciated all the references, but in my notes, there it was staring at me. This great historical thinker wrote about the dangers of how we think of wants and needs. The root of the problem is evident when we compare ourselves to others and we think we should be more like them. This goes against self-love that Rousseau spoke of; the same concept that Louise Hay has dedicated her life's work to. If you go against self-love this is the real selfishness. We need to avoid this as teachers and see in our students when they are behaving the way they do because they are comparing and competing. In that same course, we learned about Zen Masters and learning and teaching v. actual schooling. One Zen Master used stories and metaphors to provide insight. Not technical mastery but enlightenment. The master was helpful in an indirect way. Here, the role of the teacher was to guide and to care for the student and their learning experience. The teacher addresses the whole person as they learn. There is an affirmation for us all. "I address the whole person as they learn."

Then there was the course "Psychology of Education." Ah yes, Skinner, Bloom and Maslow. Here is where I learned, but only now fully comprehend, that everything teachers do is colored by the psychology theory (of learning) they hold. Teachers who do not make sense to their students and make use of a systematic body of theory in their day to day decisions are behaving blindly. I know that now because I've been there and done that. Such teachers make little more than busy-work assignments. And students see through this. This same course taught us about humanist standpoints in education. This is affirmation-based pedagogy peeking its head out. Humanists propose that students learn more effectively when they don't feel threatened in the school environment and when the messages they receive about involvement in schools helps them foster a positive self-concept.

Humanist educators like to create a positive climate in which students:

a) feel accepted and respected as people of value and worth

b) are able to express their opinions, feelings, and identities openly

c) know that they can make mistakes without being identified as failures

d) see that the knowledge they bring from home is validated in the curriculum.

Humanist psychology dictates that teachers should implement the following strategies:

a) be honest with students

b) communicate acceptance and create a sense of community

c) hold students accountable for achieving goals yet not place them under surveillance.

d) Provide meaningful tasks for students to do that relate to their own lives

e) Ask fewer questions with "right" answers and ask more open ended questions

f) Give students a sense of control

g) Establish limits and present them as informational rather then as forms of control

Then, we have the classroom management course. How quickly teachers forget the four commandments of dealing with parents:

1. understanding

2. regular communication

3. listen to what the parent is saying

4. do not pass judgment

I don't know about you, but I've been guilty of that last one more than anything. To be guilty of that is a hefty negative affirmation. As an exercise, pause now before reading further, and go back to the fifteen points under the three sub sections above and convert them into affirmations, for example, "I release the need to pass judgment on parents" or "I strive with all my energy to provide meaningful tasks for students to do that relate to their own lives."

Now, here's some more for you to convert. The top ten key characteristics of a lesson plan (if you don't use lesson plans, you have to ask yourself, what are you doing? Winging it?? What are you affirming?):

a) introduction/ice breaker/overview/sequence/group activity

b) timing

c) instructions

d) content

e) structure

f) Q & A

g) Materials/resources

h) Objectives/goals

i) Back-up plan

j) Target all learners

Now, I see in my notes a list of "Don't's". Take a moment to convert them into affirmations. Don't:

- criticize in public
- get mad when you get advise
- assume
- wing it
- use sarcasm
- criticize a student in the staff room
- adopt an attitude where you do not want to get to know your students

Example affirmations:

-I use specific praise

-humility is OK

-I communicate often and avoid surprises

-I PLAN! PLAN! PLAN!

-I share my sense of caring and humor

-I review records/consult with others

-Occasionally, I rock my students' world and they rock mine

-I teach well, guide well, instruct very well and facilitate exceptionally

-I set an example

-I make students think

-I motivate

-I mentor/role model

-I refrain from becoming attached

-I can make a learning opportunity out of absolutely anything

-I work to increase literacy and basic skills in my community

-I infuse within my students a love of learning

-I am passionate about knowledge

-I do my job because I love it

-Everyone I work with daily is very capable and effective

-I honor diversity

-I believe intolerance comes from ignorance and that education can wipe it out

-I am tirelessly creative

It is a good idea to network with other teachers and exchange affirmations. A great place to do this is on-line. For example, those of you with Facebook will find that there are teacher affirmations groups and applications. I have a Facebook group called "Teachers Rule" where people can post affirmations and share ideas and links.

Students will not all find their way to the vortex by the time you are done with them, not on their own. It is futile to think otherwise; it is an impossibility. But you can affirm to be consistent, fair, and positive. Remember, if we do try to punish students into the vortex we can be doing serious harm to them because we are teaching them the wrong thing and anytime we do this it can be detrimental to their learning or even to their health. It has been stated in the book *It's the Thought That Counts* that our thoughts can affect our genes and how we learn has an effect on how we think. "...our thoughts and feelings produce significant biological differences between us. Learning has been proven to do this in which genes are on and which are off, which in turn lead to differences in the growth of the brain and differences in the body due to the bodymind connection."

CHAPTER 12

MINDFULNESS

As society recognizes that thoughts and emotions are powerful modulators of our biological codes, new educational systems will arise to teach people how to control their emotions and thoughts through self-regulated bio feedback.

-Karl Maret, M.D.-

In the middle of the book, *The Power,* I was struck by the words: "If you are walking down the street listening to the thoughts in your head, you miss it all." I was frozen there on that spot on the page realizing that I really do like to listen to my own thoughts and often do miss out on taking in the beauty around me which means I am not as mindful as I want to be nor am I as mindful as I want, need, and expect my students to be!

Mindfulness is being of aware of our thoughts. When we are not, we attract things we do not want into our lives. We will discuss this in greater detail in the luck chapter, but it is summed up best in *The Power*: "Everything in the universe is magnetic and everything has a magnetic frequency. Your feelings and thoughts have magnetic frequencies too. Good feelings mean you're on a positive frequency of love." It's no wonder why athletes and teams get rattled in sports otherwise there would be no blow-outs in sports. Mindfulness is being aware that all our affirmations are connected. I may want to infuse within my students a love of learning History let's say, because I know that I myself love History and can make it exciting and not boring. Although, if I feel I have no energy than since I need energy, my affirmation is negative not positive. It's the same way in life, for instance, I love to travel and yet I have not travelled much despite feeling only positive feelings about travelling, I have had money problems for several years, not so much the student-debt and maxed-out credit cards and consolidation loans, but I have always felt negative about money, thinking I never had enough to keep up. I no longer choose this reality and I have been travelling more as of late.

Furthermore, The University of Windsor defines mindfulness as: "Mindfulness is the core teaching of Guatama Buddha. Thich Nhat Hanh, a Vietnamese Zen Buddhist monk in exile, a peace activist who was nominated by Martin Luther King Jr. for the Nobel Peace Prize, tells a story which best illustrates the meaning of mindfulness. Once Guatama Buddha was asked, "What do you and your students practice?" He replied, "We sit, we walk, and we eat." The questioner continued, 'But everyone sits, walks, and eats." The Buddha then said, "When we sit, we know we are sitting. When we walk, we know we are walking. When we eat, we know we are eating." School work would fall under sitting here in terms of mindfulness but the problem in getting the concepts of mindfulness into the classrooms. It may be even a bigger problem if the school is Catholic, religious, or private where the school(s) may be under the misconception that it will lead to the use of terms like "metaphysical" which could lead to a fear that it might be anti-religious or go against religious teachings, this is not true though. I am Catholic. Interestingly, when I attended the Louis Hay "I Can Do It Conference" 2010 in Toronto, Dr. Wayne Dyer spent most of his time speaking of St. Padre Pio and St. Francis of Assisi and the stigmata. Religion and/or spirituality and mindfulness do go together. In public schools, the fear might be that it is too religious. However, mindfulness in and of itself has little to do with religion. In recent years, many practitioners in the health and mental health field have adopted the practice of mindfulness in working with clients with chronic pain, stress, depression, and other psychological distress. Mindfulness is about being here, fully present with all our activities and thoughts, with body and mind united. If you are at work feeling stressed, tired, apathetic, or frustrated you are not as efficient as you could be and you can scale back on the amount of these types of days that you have. It's all about nurturing awareness, clarity, and openness to present-moment experiences.

Kids are wonderful. Teaching is a noble and fun profession. Right? Read those two statements again. They are positive affirmations. Why do so many teachers not affirm this? It is a vocation. The sad reality can't be ignored that many teachers do not consider it a profession. I have been in the staff room when a teacher says "Teaching is not a vocation, that's just something teachers say to make themselves feel better, teaching is just a job." And this gets said in a room filled with teachers, most of who, if not all of whom, disagree with this perception, but none of whom interject to filter this flawed statement. If you believe that teaching is just a job then this is what you affirm and you will always be limited as a teacher. Similarly, there are teachers who are too authoritarian who are too hard on their students are thus inadvertently inviting parents to phone or write their principal, board, board of trustees, college of teachers, and/or Ministry of Education to vent and give flack making that teacher's life a sea of frustration. Or even worse, there are even more teachers who are much too permissive and who not only have no intention or desire to enforce school rules, they actually are critical of those teachers that do. A classic example is a teacher openly says that s/he will not breakup a fight when and if one breaks out on their watch citing the rule that teachers can't touch students. Take something as simple as dress code and cell phones/I-pods policies. Teachers who encourage their students to defy these rules need to ask themselves, why are they so against these rules? Do they think it saves on behavior management? If so, at what cost? Do they think the rule(s) are fundamentally flawed and they themselves are beacons of superior classroom policy? If so, why not tell their administrators how they feel as opposed to giving the impression that they do in fact enforce rules. This kind of misleading is counter-productive. It does not solve any issues. Negative affirmations can be solutions.

I myself have experienced being both too permissive and being too authoritarian. And in both cases, it was a result of my not being patient or present in the moment. If I am not being patient I am not being mindful. Patience always increases with the use of affirmations.

If I am not mindful, I lose rapport. Animosity is the opposite of good rapport. It is immature to have a lack of rapport with students. Here is a rapport quiz score-finder. Try it out.

Yes No 1. Do you lose your temper at any time?

2. Do you always give your student equal consideration with yourself?

3. Do you criticize your student(s) in the presence of other people?

4. Do you ever sulk, complain, or grieve, when you don't get your own way?

5. Do you worry?

Side-note: Mindfulness eliminates the need to worry. Remember the song, "Don't Worry Be Happy?" It is fundamentally true. Or, a better example: when I was in university, there was a popular song on the radio called "Everyone is Free to Wear Sunscreen" which had a line that said, "Don't worry about the future, or worry but know that worrying is about as effective as trying to solve an algebra equation by chewing bubble gum."

6. Do you affirm, have faith in yourself, and try your best?

7. Do you accept the ups and downs of life

8. Do you have conviction?

Side-note: what is meant by conviction? When CBC's *The Hour*'s George Strombolopolis interviewed former Prime Minister, the Right Honorable Paul Martin, he asked him "what do you first and foremost need to be Prime Minister?" Mr. Martin replied, "Conviction." Conviction is important, a true leader knows that s/he can meet and solve problems.

Results: Yes to 1, 3, 4, 5 indicate immaturity. Yes to the others are to be equated with a mature personality. Since 99% of you at least answered 'yes' to #3, the next step is to improve your score through affirmations. It is true that affirmations tend to work best if you believe in them. Affirmations do work and can be used by anyone. To think otherwise means that you have an unimaginative mind, such minds through the generations said the world can't possibly be round, the earth must be the centre of the universe, we are out of inventions, man will never fly, radios will never be in automobiles, and 'land on the moon?' 'preposterous!' It's not telepathy, precognition, or clairvoyance we're talking here, though those do exist and are absolutely amazing to research and study and serve as further evidence of greater capacities within us all to stronger more effective lives; it is affirmations i.e., communicating in consistent positive language. It is a simple concept that can not be debunked. Believe me I have tried to debunk all this when I thought that they did not work. Google: "affirmations don't work" or "Affirmations are a waste of time" you won't find anything to support that.

But it does work. We tend to think that it does not work because so much literature on positive affirmations like *The Secret* make it sound like it is a way to eliminate all problems in life. While it is true that a dedication to positive affirmations leads to a glaring lack of defeat, failure, and hopelessness in life, life is not easy, life is life, it is real and it is full of problems. You can master your problems. And that is the difference.

Affirmations are more than just words. When children play they are affirming positivity. Imagine denying a child of play. What kind of adult do you think they would be? In the fascinating book, *Play-How It Shapes the Brain, Opens the Imagination, and invigorates the Soul,* by Stuart Brown, there is an in-depth correlation between play and success. In other words, the more children play, the better. When children play they are emitting positive energy to themselves and those around them. It might be a red flag when an adult despite being in the presence of a playing child/children/student(s), is impatient or stressed (etc). But it isn't a book about children, it's a book for all of us. In *Star Trek* the Vulcan race suppress their emotions to have more reason and logic in their lives, there is no time for play because it is lacking in purpose. We are not Vulcans! The reality is we all need to expose ourselves to what entertains us. In terms of how this relates to the classroom, learning and memory are connected to play. Brown says, "Learning itself is enhanced by play, as many teachers know- which is why classrooms often use role play or simulation to teach a subject that is difficult or perceived to be boring." Affirm that your classes will not be boring, but phrase it in a positive way i.e. "my lessons will be exciting enough for my students to learn and look forward to subsequent learning." The book *Play* clearly shows a connection between play and neural connections, also: "There is a great deal of evidence that the road to mastery of any subject is guided by play."

As I said though, life isn't all fun and games. After play, self-reliance is a positive affirmation. Affirm that your students learn self-reliance. This is the mark of a great teacher. As Brown goes on to state, "Some parents don't allow kids the independence necessary for them to learn self-reliance" referring to parents who write their kids research papers for them (etc). I remember taking academic or advanced French when I was in grade nine thinking that I came from a long line of French Canadians and I could handle it. But I barely passed. I remember the teacher one day scolding me for turning in homework that my mother had done for me which was obvious to her because I was conjugating verbs that not even her grade thirteen students knew. In grade ten I took French at the general or applied level with the same teacher and got a high mark without the help of my mother. Of course I stopped taking French after that because it was no longer mandatory. In many ways I regret not having learned to speak it fluently. If I set my mind to it, I know I could still pick it up in a year (or any language for that matter). Maybe I will yet; everyone has a list of things to do or try in their life, some will never get their checklist completed because they affirm that these goals will only be accomplished "someday" (as Credence Clearwater Revival said, "someday never comes."). Those who use affirmations actually get to everything on the list. New Years Resolutions work for them too.

When I was in Teachers' College, one of my host teachers turned out to be my former teacher who had taught me History and English, and to me then and now, he is a guru and the coolest teacher you could ask for, told me or warned me that some days this job is a lot of fun and other days it's AWFUL. In retrospect, he was absolutely right. Why is this? Does it have to be like this? I heard a teacher ask a principal once if they were happy at the school despite "all the nonsense" and the principal replied, "there's more good days than bad." That's a start.

We have to enjoy our work and enjoy it often. I regret all the days I worked that I was tired and feeling indifferent for it was a disservice to my students on my part. But then there is the issue of regret. Regret is unhealthy so we can use affirmations to forgive ourselves.

Play author Brown puts it well in his book, "We can have fun. We can discover how to find as much joy as we do when involved in any project, as much joy as we did when we were a kid making paper airplanes and flying them from the roof."

I never made paper airplanes as a kid. Next to math, art was my worst subject (another subject my one "bad" principal made me teach), but I do recall my obsession with professional wrestling, I had more wrestling figures than any kid in my town. Just writing about it now brings back good memories. This is a feeling of lightness and essentially is a form of meditation which by now we all know is extremely healthy both mentally and physically.

It's about time schools starting having meditation though it is still scarce. Some students get chances to meditate in school in physical health education or Religion. We are seeing more and more of this. I have tried it in religion classes and my IDC4O (Mindful Healthy Living) class and the students absolutely love it. I even have them make theor own meditations and they love it.

If you had chronic pain of some sort you would see a doctor or go to the hospital, why would you want to ignore the problem of a lack of feelings of lightness in your life? Light up your classroom with positive energy and you will have little to complain about. When you have lots of energy you don't tend to complain. Talk to your principal and include in your Annual Learning Plan ways to bring "play" to your classroom. Take them outside (if you are allowed). Give them a lecture break. Reward them with PAT points (preferred activity time), give them stretch breaks. If someone does an oral presentation on video games allow them to bring their X-Box in for the class to enjoy (Rated "E" for everyone games of course), get a guest speaker, go on a field trip, have a pizza with them at lunch. This counts as differentiated instruction too.

Play author, Stuart goes on to state, "Even a short walk can lift the spirits. The body remembers what the mind has forgotten. Body play is the first thing that shows up in evolution... When people are able to find that sense of play in their work, they become truly powerful figures. It can be transformative."

In the books, *Sway- the Irresistible Pull of Irrational Behavior* by Ori Brafman and Rom Brafman and *How We Decide* by Jonah Lehrer, we learn to have more empathy for people in times of poor decisions. If only we could sit down with people we know and say, "read this book" or "this book I read says...." It doesn't work like that. There seems to be very little that we can do to change the decisions our friends make in their lives, it's a matter of neuroscience. Not as bleak though for the student-teacher relationship.

Remember, the teacher is wielding authority and can more easily impress upon a student. We learn best from our mistakes. So teachers have a great opportunity to give positive affirmative mindful feedback to students that will have a huge positive impact on their lives. Never before in the history of education has such an emphasis been put on report card comments, especially at the elementary level. For some reason, there are no report card comments at the post-secondary level which is unfortunate. It is based on the reality that students care about their mark and don't always look at the comment, so too can be said for many parents. I can count on one hand the amount of time a parent came into an interview and took out the report card and asked about a comment and even in those times it was usually to argue that the comment was inaccurate when it certainly wasn't in my professional judgment. These report card comments which list a strength, a weakness, and a next step are often ignored by the reader because they have to be or tend to be in official curriculum expectations mumbo-jumbo. Don't get me wrong, report cards are to be taken seriously, I always spend several days working on them whereas I know some teachers complete them in less than three hours, or less. I don't know if I should be impressed or disappointed, I guess it depends. The report card and the comment should be completely separate. The comments should be a one page letter attached to a learning skills rubric. And assignments should have feedback on it phrased carefully. "You must have worked hard on this" as it turns out through actual studies is much more effective than "Wow, you must be smart." The first makes the student feel challenged and up for future challenges. The latter, leads to the student being satisfied with minimum expectations. Again, it's a matter of language and neuroscience. However, it is good to see that in the province of Ontario, the Ministry of Education has instructed educators to use laymen's terms and personalize report card comments. You can still do this and use report card comment banks of course.

What is profound for teachers to know as Brafman states, "...we can't help but take on the characteristics others ascribe to us...we're all psychological chameleons. So, if your students start thinking of you as a pushover or easy marker or hard marker or unorganized or mean or cool or strict (etc), this will spread into the mindset of you, co-workers, other students, and their parents. You have the power to tweak all of these to be positive by believing just that. Furthermore, in Lehrer's book, we learn all about loss aversion theory and negative bias. It is important for teachers to begin to realize that "it generally takes at least five kind comments to compensate for one critical comment."

Car accidents are the leading cause of death for those under the age of twenty-one. *How We* Decide author Jonah Lehrer states, "Teens make bad decisions because they are literally less rational." But he makes a paramount side-note in showing that there are ways to compensate for the irrational brains of teens. So, never give up on a troubled teen.

It's easy to know what mindfulness is and not so easy to always know what it isn't. In 2010, my school implemented a new discipline system whereby a student could no longer be sent to the office, s/he must first be sent to a "classroom buddy." Let me explain for those of you who do not know what this system entails. It means you are responsible to pick two co-workers that will act as a classroom buddy in the event you need to eject a student, you must sent them there first. If they misbehave there, they can be sent to the student support worker and then, and only then, if they misbehave they can be sent to the office and/or suspended. It is mindful to say that this is being implemented because it has been productive and effective elsewhere and it is an honor if a teacher sends someone to your class because that means they trust that you will be able to control that student better than you can (I suppose in theory, a teacher could send a student to a class that was already difficult and had a teacher least likely to control that student just to increase the chance that student would find themselves in more trouble but to do so would be a conspiracy and thus a negative affirmation!). However, when this came out I noticed that I and most of my co-workers complained that it was unfair, that some people would never have a student sent to them and others would have to take a student that was not theirs on a frequent basis. A better example is how we perceive students who are labeled as behavior issues. There is nothing mindful about that as far as I can tell. Remember the scene in *Problem Child* where Gilbert Godfrey's character says: "OK, you want a little kid, well, all kids are little, today, I came across this seven-year- old; he's a little rambunctious, but weren't we all at that age." And John Ritter's character adopts Junior and he doesn't take long before he says, "We've adopted Satan." But the audience is rooting for Junior the whole time and at the end you come to know his unfortunate dysfunctional past that has led to him being such behavior concern and when he and his new family are settled in he turns out to be a great kid after all.

The benefits of mindfulness could be listed over many pages but for us teachers, they include less stress, improved focus and awareness, increasing responsiveness to students' needs, promoting of emotional balance, supporting of healthy relationships at work and home, enhancing of classroom climate, and supporting of overall well-being.

CHAPTER 13

WHAT AM I AFFIRMING?

Sometimes we chose not to know things because we can anticipate that they would have an uncontrollable effect on our emotions.

-Steven Pinker-

This opening above quote comes from Steven Pinker's *The Stuff of Thought* which is not a book about affirmations but a book on language (any English teacher would love this book), but it does not have to be so. Pinker says most of would rather not know the day on which we will die, which is true but again, this does not have to be so. If we are to be at peace, we really are to be at peace that we are going to leave this planet someday. I've often thought about whether or not I would want to know my "death-day" but that's not the point. The point is what you are affirming determines what level of peace you have in your life.

I remember the first time I played *Mario-Kart* on the *Wii* and did very poorly and went on a rant about how pointless and unhealthy video games were! Afterward, when I calmed down, I realized how unreasonable I was and took several days to keep playing the game until I was good at it. To this day, I absolutely love to play it. Likewise, when I played *Guitar Hero* for the first time, I thought that the game was totally unfair because I did poorly at it. I asked, "how can anyone think this is fun!?" But then I tried the Aerosmith version of the game and being a huge fan of the band, I put all my effort into it and to this day, I adore the game. How I can hate something one day and love it the next, or someone for that matter, all has to do with thought-energy.

Studies show that we have 60,000 thoughts a day on average and over 90% of them are the same thoughts as we had yesterday. What did you affirm today? If something positive, why not keep that flow going into tomorrow? It's not the easiest thing to do. It is like trying to lose weight, there are lots of diets and de-toxes that get the job done, some are healthier than others and none of them are easy, though they certainly seem easier with the use of affirmations.

What you can do is affirm that if the emotional brain is pointing you in the direction of a bad decision, you can choose to rely on your rational brain instead; affirm that you will find ways to effectively teach this life skill to your students.

Affirm that you are in it for the students. Everything else will fall into place. This means making your peace with the fact that teaching is often a thankless job. In the book *The School Solution* by Paul Kropp and Lynda Hodson, we get a sense of the reality as well articulated in the following quote, "...Even our (media), which once applauded teachers for the nobility of their calling, have now taken to blaming them for everything from declining test scores to violence in the school parking lot. It's a shame. There are many, many good teachers out there and quite a few excellent ones, all working little miracles despite declining budgets, fragmenting families, TV-inspired violence, mouthy students and a host of societal contradictions that can pull a good teacher apart. Just when more kids need a hug than ever before- and are less likely to get one at home- our teachers can be charged for putting an arm around a student..."

Being a teacher is all about overcoming these downsides. In the same book, there is a 'What to Look For" checklist for parents to tell if their child's teacher is a poor teacher. So take note and make sure this is not you and make sure you affirm that you are a good teacher and affirm you avoid these characteristics: homework is busywork or nonexistent; marking is done late (why would a teacher hand something back more than a week after it was handed in? I admit I am guilty of having done this but realize it was selfish of me to do so); record keeping is spotty or lost (some teacher shave been knows to lose culminating tasks or final exams (I once had a class not return seven of their text books and more of them would have returned these had I been using affirmations, instead I was embarrassed because my department head jokingly accused me of selling them and pocketing the money. At least I think he was joking. I'm not sure, but the fact that seven students did not return their books was ultimately my procrastination to not collect them properly and call the parents of those students who did not return a book, by the way, you should affirm that your students all have a book, that same book is their assigned book and that they return them); the class is frequently out of control; even 'good' students are given detentions (though not every star pupil who gets a detention is serving an unwarranted detention, when I was in grade eleven, I served my one and only detention because I was late for class because I was talking to a girl that I had a huge crush on. I think it was worth it); the teacher is frequently sick or away from the class (I think teachers should not abuse their sick days nor do I think they should get a reward for never having taken a sick day. I've never gone a year where I didn't take a sick day. You probably earn yourself at least one mental health sick day a semester. If you are out of the class for PD, this is a smart choice in the long run, simply send a monthly newsletter home that explains this to parents so they don't think you are setting a bad example and when it comes to PD, always tell your students either before or after where you were and why); finally, there is lots of attention to form rather than learning.

Many parents think that teachers are vengeful creatures, which is as wrong as the public perception that teachers always have summers off (when in reality of course, for any non-teachers reading this, teachers have to prepare for September, take courses and teach summer school). So affirm that you project the opposite of the stereotypes.

In Carol Ann Tomlinson's book *How to Differentiate Instruction in Mixed-Ability Classrooms*, we can see the importance of subtle differences in classroom atmospheres. "The tone of any classroom greatly affects those who inhabit it and the learning that takes place there. Classroom environment in a setting that strives for differentiation is, if anything, even more of a factor in shaping success." Therefore, affirm that everyone feels welcomed and contributes to everyone else feeling welcomed. Affirm that there is a pervasive expectation of growth ("The goal in a differentiated classroom is to help every learner grow as much as he or she can in both general ability and specific talents. The teacher gets excited about the growth of each individual learner.").

Don't say "I don't care what people think." This is a philosophy that time and time again has proven ineffective. We are social creatures. Leadership Lane's "Master Teacher" vol.34/Number 12 "The Verbal Habits That Undermine Your Image" states that "...what others think is vitally important." It is sometimes OK to laugh at our own mistakes. I used to spend a great deal of time with my friends and siblings making fun of my luck. I could have written 100 SNL skits based on the shtick I was producing. I was told by an Akeshic records reader that I had to stop doing this. "...the continual use of self-effacing comments or putdowns can cause students and colleagues to question our ability and competence. It's difficult for others to have confidence in themselves" ("Master Teacher"). "Blaming anyone on the school team for a problem is a mistake." Pointing blame does not fix a problem and makes you feel even more stressed and powerless. I spent several years as the Student Council Advisor and one year in particular the person who won the presidency was someone I knew had no leadership skills. I wanted to rig the election. I tried to convince the principal to demote her because she wasn't doing anything. In retrospect, the school-spirit may have been mediocre with or without her, but would have been more memorable and eventful in a positive way had I have been more supportive, open-minded, and proactive. I think I let down my principal that year the same way the Student Council president in question let me down. Some disappointments are a self-fulfilling prophecy.

In Steven Pinker's book, *The Stuff of Thought,* the author uses the study of language to illustrate that it's not just teachers, but everyone on the planet that needs to be open to new ideas in how we communicate and manage our lives. So when we ask ourselves what it is that we are affirming... we must consider what we are saying, the words and tone we use and certainly what we are thinking. In terms of education, Pinker states: "The goal of education is to make up for the shortcomings in our instinctive ways of thinking about the physical and social world. And education is likely to succeed not by trying to implant abstract statements in empty minds but by taking the mental models that our standard equipment, applying them to new subjects in selective analogies, and assembling them into new and more sophisticated combinations."

So what are you affirming and what should you be affirming? Here are some beneficial affirmations to help your students be better students and thereby make your job far less stressful:

-I support "readiness to learn"

-I promote academic performance

-I promote strengthening of attention and concentration in my classroom

-I reduce anxiety before testing and culminating tasks in my classroom

-I always promote self-reflection

-My students are calm

-I find ways to improve classroom participation

-Pro-social behaviors are fostered in my classroom

-I practice mindful breathing on the job

-When I wake up, I wake up mindfully so my day is sure to meet or exceed expectations

-I aspire to express more patience today

-If I am calm, my students will instinctively move toward their own sense of calm

-If I treat my students with respect and integrity, they are likely to return the courtesy

CHAPTER 14

AFFIRMATIONS WHEN THE GAS LIGHT COMES ON

Whenever I'm teaching a group an introduction to affirmations, I always say, you can't use affirmations to win the lottery (that's what Louise Hay calls "poverty thinking") and you can't drive and see your gas light come on and think that you won't run out of gas. The point being that if the gas light comes on it's too late, you weren't mindful in the first place. Now, you can hope that you make it to a gas station before you run out of a gas which is a stressful experience.

Is it positive affirmations that work or is it that negative thinking does what it does and positive affirmations just represent a lack of negative thoughts and thereby more inner peace in life? Does it matter? In any event, it works. This does not give you a license to live your life as a Mr. or Mrs. Teacher from 9 to 5 and then Mr. or Mrs. Social Butterfly Party Animal the rest of the time mistakenly thinking that pictures of your three sick days spent in Vegas including the hot tub party you posted on Facebook will not fall into the wrong hands because your thoughts will deter it and prevent it from ever happening. You've got the theory wrong. In actual fact, such behavior is destructive in that it is inviting just that. Having said that, Facebook is not in and of itself a negative thing. I remember taking pictures at one year-end staff party and one staff member clearly complaining that she was in no uncertain terms not to be in any pictures that went on Facebook, and that "Facebook ruins lives." What she fails to realize is that she is implying by deduction that these people whose lives have been ruined by Facebook would be doing just fine if it wasn't for Facebook. This is wrong. With or without Facebook, they would be having similar levels of dysfunction or heartache or stress in their lives. The Ontario College of Teachers publishes *Professional Speaking* to all its members several times a year (a professional development magazine for teachers and administrators). In the June 2009 edition, there was a feature article, "Can We Be Friends" by Stuart Foxman that strongly opposed Facebook and warned teachers not to use it. It cited several examples from across North America of teachers being reprimanded for their Facebook content. It even warned student teachers: "In one Missouri school district , a superintendent has been known to ask teaching candidates if they have a Facebook or MyPage page. If the answer is yes, the superintendent says, "I've got my computer up right now- let's take a look." This of course is scare-tactics. Teachers need not live their lives in fear. Common sense already tells you not to add a student to Facebook or reply to a student that messages you on Facebook lest you give that student access to your profile. There's certainly nothing wrong with not having Facebook. It's a good rule of thumb not to have anything on there that belittles students because that would be hard to defend and more importantly, it would already be sending out the wrong affirmation about how you view the profession even if you were the only one looking at your profile (indeed, I saw a Facebook documentary once where a teacher was fired because she posted a rant on Facebook calling her students "germ-bags."). It is sometimes OK to consider accepting friend requests from former students but only after they have graduated and moved on and you feel a level of trust. Facebook has agreed to let third party advertisers use your posted pictures without your permission. Click on "Settings" up at the top where you see the "Logout" link. Select "Privacy". Then select "News Feed and Wall". Next, select the tab that reads "Facebook Ads". In the drop down box, select "No One". Then save your changes.

There is a difference between being stressed-out and overwhelmed in September versus June. In June, a lot of the stress may go back to my gas light analogy. If I had to describe my job in one word I would use the word busy. A teacher is overwhelmed with work when report card deadline week is upon them but even on back to back snow days, there is always something to do. I strongly urge teachers to affirm that the more busy you are, the more things get done. This is literally true, so look at it from that perspective and be happy while being busy as opposed to being stressed. It will have a complete opposite effect on your physical health too, it's a way of thinking that is an anti-venom. As "The Master Teacher Volume 34 Edition 1 Number 23 states: " Anyone who has taught for any length of time knows that one of the most difficult aspects of teaching is that the better you are, the more you know how much more you need to know- and how much more needs to be done... education must work for us as well as for students if we are to work at optimum levels of effectiveness. Unfortunately, there's no magic formula we can follow that will guarantee we are healthy and energized all the time (But this goes back to realizing that being outside the vortex leads to expansion). But there are some things we can do to take care of ourselves." It goes on to talk about the benefits of meditation. Most teachers do not meditate. Obviously, some teachers medicate. More teachers are on anti-depressants than most professionals. And it is debatable as to what percentage of the time such medication works. But this is one of the main reasons teachers should be in a union (for the support available) which I promise we will get more into. Our planning must allow time for us to do things for ourselves. We need and deserve the best of care. Teachers or anyone else, who have crossed the line from happy most of the time to unhappy most of the time have lost sight of their super capacity as a human to change their situation dramatically, in fact according to *The Power*, "You can change your frequency at any time by changing how you feel, and everything around you will change because you're on a new frequency."

I love the analogy of the glass of water in *The Power*. We all know about the glass half full v. half empty debate but just as we certainly can't change the emptiness of a glass of water with just a little bit of water at the bottom by complaining about the lack of water, we can't change negativity and bad luck by complaining and swearing or saying "this isn't happening... this isn't happening." These are the times when affirmations won't work because they can't work. It would be like your body being dehydrated and you trying to hydrate yourself without actually drinking any water. It won't happen because it can't happen. If you get into the habit of using affirmations at school they will work and gone will be the days where you contemplate leaving the profession and gone will be the days of your name appearing on Rate My Teacher Dot Com. Speaking of RMT.com (or ratemyprofessers.com), first of all, let's be clear, ratemyteacher.com is run by an anti-teacher organization. It is bias to the point that it is irrelevant and, one could argue, should be illegal. In any event, the company is international now and doesn't lose sleep at night thinking that they are proving a public service. They like to state that most of the ratings are positive and that slanderous comments are removed by moderators. Both claims are false. There are other similar sites too, many of these websites do not monitor or filter the content or comments posted by the students that use them. Further, these services offer students a level of anonymity that may lead to a diminished sense of culpability. The result is that some of the comments and/or content posted on these websites constitute rudeness, or are hurtful, and even defamatory. Historically, when a person was the subject of an offensive and/or defamatory publication, that person could sue the publisher and the author of the defamatory content. Today, the Internet has added a new level of complexity to this course of action. Many websites are run from servers located outside of Canada or the USA and the operators can be very difficult to locate. Nevertheless, victims of offensive or defamatory postings have avenues of recourse aside from civil litigation.

Most reputable websites and social networking services, such as Facebook and MySpace, have policies in place to ensure that any offensive or defamatory postings can be removed as soon as they are brought to the attention of the service operators. Postings on other websites, like ratemyteacher.com, can be more difficult to remove. This type of website actively encourages students to post comments about their teachers and their policies state that they will remove comments only in extreme cases. Also, www.ratemyteacher.com does not offer an easy to use content removal procedure. However, despite these variances between website policies, it is generally understood that offensive or defamatory content should be removed once discovered and brought to the attention of the appropriate managers. One good thing is that less students use RMT now because they can use Facebook applications and groups instead. Teachers and parents have access to RMT but not the Facebook applications and groups students are using.

Many students who love their learning experiences feel no need to go to the RMT website whereas vindictive students will find the time to unfairly rate teachers all "1" in all the categories in an extreme act of selfishness. If there are boards that use this site to monitor teachers and I'm sure there are, it is embarrassing. There are also teachers who have no business being teachers because they cross the line from professional to very inappropriate and yet pass with flying colors and get full marks at ratemyteacher.com. The unions should lobby the government to eliminate this website, though even if this were to happen, more students, as I mentioned, are using Facebook groups and applications to rate teachers where the ratings can't be viewed by the public. However, since it is there you might as well look over your rating to make sure that you are "passing" and if not you need to make sure this isn't just the work of vindictive students. Take my ratings for example: At my old school: # of Ratings 9; Average Easiness: 4.2; Average Helpfulness: 4.2; Average Clarity: 4.3; Popularity Total: 7; Overall Quality: 4.3. Not bad. Though notice there are only 9 ratings and during my four years there I would have taught some 130 students. My former principal who I complained about earlier is also listed there, she did not fair as well. I never said Ratemyteacher.com was always inaccurate. And then at my next school: # of Ratings 15; Average Easiness: 4.1; Average Helpfulness: 3.6; Average Clarity: 3.6; Popularity Total: 10; Overall Quality: 3.6. I look at that and think 3.6!! You got to be kidding me! It should be at least 4! But again, here we have fifteen ratings and in those three years I would have taught around 300 students. Several students just log into the site and click all 1's. The "I'll show him" attitude. At first glance, you would feel resentment towards such a student (There was one comment in particular on mine that admitted bias, "I blame him for my English marks in gr. 11 and 12." I had taught this student in grade ten.) but in actual fact they wouldn't be circling all 1's if they were honest and truthful, they have a lot of negativity and rated other teachers poorly and unfairly as well and probably over-rated the few or one teacher(s) they did enjoy having and this warrants compassion not resentment. And I know that had I have been using positive affirmations back then, there would be less of these annoying ratings. I would say out of all the classes I have ever taught the ones who I felt learned the most and were most connected to me were my students at Algonquin College in 2009 who all gave me very impressive feedback on the midterm and final evaluation forms though at ratemyprofessers.com I do not yet exist. Needless to say I do not support the existence of RMT but for the most part, the teachers who have negative ratings on the site have attracted that reality into their lives according to the law of attraction which leads into the following chapter.

CHAPTER 15

LAW OF ATTRACTION

You can see by now how important it is to really connect with all our students. Michael J. Losier wrote *The Law of Connection* and after reading it, I realized how much easier my job would be and how much more joyous it would be if I learned how to have an excellent rapport with all of my students and co-workers instead of just a few. Any teacher can have a good rapport with some of their students. This happens naturally. But we need to pick up on verbal cues of everyone else and make a conscious effort to do so. Losier calls this "calibrating" which builds rapport. I use this book as the text book for my IDC4O Mindful Healthy Living course.

I don't know how many times I put on a report card: "Johnny needs to work on his communication skills." You can say that about anyone at any time. Losier states: "Understanding other people's styles allows you to see why they receive and communicate information the way that they do. Having that information will allow you to be flexible and calibrate your communication style so that you create rapport and improve `your connections with all different types of communicators."

Even before a teacher goes to Teachers College, they know that there are different types of learners: visual, auditory, kinesthetic, (and now, digital too).

But these are also types of communicators. You should affirm that you build rapport and connect with all communication/learning styles by becoming increasingly aware of which type each person you encounter is. Anyone who has researched the "Law of Attraction" knows the benefits of this.

I highly recommend that all teachers read *The Law of Connection* because it dedicates a great deal of analysis on the various styles of communication and offers a build rapport v. breaks rapport column checklist for each of the four types and also for each type, how to ask questions that stimulate answers which is something we should also affirm if we do not want our classrooms to be boring. The premise of the book is as vital as it is simple: "The more positively we communicate, the better we connect, and the more likely we are to receive a positive response."

We can use prayer to put the law of attraction in perspective. As a Catholic, I have always prayed. Prayer illustrates the "Law of Attraction" on many levels. I admit that I have rarely noticed answered prayers in my life. This is not a contradiction, on the contrary, it proves my point when I think of how my prayers were phrased. And when I first read *The Secret* in 2007 my life fell apart and the exact opposite of my initial affirmations came true. Was I cursed? Was I doing something wrong? Or were affirmations a total hoax and a fluke coincidence for those who claimed it worked? You don't have to look far to find someone who doesn't believe in affirmations. But they do work and there is a reason why they don't when they don't. What I know now that I didn't in 2007, is thanks to the documentary *You Can Heal Your Life* by Louise Hay, and her book *I Can Do It,* which tell us that when affirmations don't work, it is because they are literally being delayed by negative thought or delayed by worry i.e., occupying your thoughts with how the affirmation(s) is going to come into your life. Hay stresses that you have to make your affirmation in present tense and in positive phrase and believe it to be true and don't worry about it. I think the last part is the most important part and the most often neglected in affirmation literature. It's "Faith 101" when you think about it. "It's not your job to figure out how to bring your affirmations to fruition. The way the Laws of Attraction work, you declare that you have something, and then the Universe brings it to you. The Universe is far more clever than you are and knows every possible way to make your affirmations come true. The only reason for delay and for seemingly denying you is that there's a part of you that doesn't believe that you deserve it. Or perhaps your beliefs are so strong that they overpower your affirmations." My first five years of teaching are an example of what she is talking about. So too my romantic life for the first thirty-two years of my life (but that is another book altogether).

Of course all a skeptic has to ask rhetorically is, "why can't you use affirmations to win the lottery?" I too used to think that way. Besides the fact that in theory you could use affirmations to win the lottery, the fact is not everyone can win the lottery and affirmations can't make something impossible possible, otherwise you could use them to fly or turn invisible. Lottery tickets can be a cheap hobby. I sometimes buy them. Louise Hay warns that affirming for lottery winnings is dangerous because it is "scarcity thinking" or "poverty thinking". You are affirming that you do not deserve the good in life you seek except by fluke. And the lottery is a fluke.

Classroom affirmations like any others won't work 100% of the time. If you are declaring: "My students are more and more submissive, attentive, and respectful," and this isn't so, then perhaps you have old, deep-seated beliefs that you don't deserve a dream classroom or more commonly your co-workers have strong negative beliefs about students, and there's a part of you that still accepts these beliefs! If you teach in an old school whose building has seen better days, the school itself may have a "pain-body" to use Eckart Tolle's terminology. All obstacles to affirmations can quickly be overcome.

There is a third obstacle to be aware of and I promise that's it. Discouragement. Many an unanswered prayer has led to loss of faith in people who were religious. But discouragement is a strong emotion that sends counter affirmations out attracting more of what you say you don't want. The summer of 2009 in eastern Ontario, upstate New York, and western Quebec was cold and rainy. By the time the summer was less than half over people were assuming that the summer was a write-off; that the remainder would be cool and wet. Since affirmations work for people they work for groups. It's a good thing that around the time of Y2K more people than not, did venture out to party and bring in the new year in a welcoming mindset. Otherwise the computers may very well have crashed. If you believe in alternate universes, I'm sure there were some universes where Y2K played out as a worst-case scenario.

There will however, come times when you are discouraged, but the more skilled you become at catching yourself doing this and changing your thinking, the easier your life becomes. You are learning a new concept. It is comparable to riding a bicycle. Why do we get back on the bike when we first take our training-wheels off and try riding ourselves and fall off as I vividly remember doing as a child? We do so because we know that we will ride that bike like everyone else and we know that if we don't get on the bike we will never be able to. For example, no matter how much you love your job you will always come across co-workers, students, administrators, and parents who you would not want to be stranded on an island with. In *The North and* South, George Hazzard and Ori Maine would never have been able to keep their friendship alive during the Civil War if not for their positive optimism and knowledge that their friendship would survive the war. The brilliant JJ Abrams show *Lost* in its first season saw a group of castaways who worked together and focused on being positive and when there were confrontations between two people they were surrounded by positive people and the confrontation dissolved. If Jack, Kate, Sun, and especially Hurley weren't on the island it may have been a *Lord of the Flies*-fest. Hurley who was a lottery-jackpot winner, found that the lottery didn't do him much good on the island and as flashbacks showed, didn't do much for him before the plane-crash either. Many lottery winners lose their winnings in two years and have little to show for it. You can take the world's most miserable person and give them a winning lottery ticket and you just have a rich cynic. There is no change in consciousness. The people on *Lost* were able to develop strategies to successfully deal with frustrating people. Their survival depended on it. Why not put more effort in this in our workplace? Over time, imagine what depends on it? "The Master Teacher" in vol.34, Num.22, states that there are strategies which will lower anxiety: you will be more successful if you listen more and refuse to form instant opinions (this is a tall order, if you read any of Malcolm Gladwell's sociological works such as *Blink*, you know that our brains are programmed to literally judge a book by its cover), lighten up and realize that when you allow people to frustrate you, you have allowed them control over you, look for common ground, don't let yourself get caught up in details and minor issues with which you disagree, and lastly, neutralize negative feelings. We don't have to like everyone either. I wouldn't go so far as to say I like my former principal even though I have forgiven her. And the reality is most of our co-workers are just that, co-workers, not friends. I enjoy my summer vacation and usually don't get to see co-workers during the summer even when I'm just on "staycation." However, to never see your co-workers outside of school can be a negative affirmation since we know that intention is powerful, it depends on your intentions. Dr. David R. Hamilton has written: "We intend things throughout the day… every one of our intentions goes somewhere. Quite likely, if we are thinking of specific people, it will be going right to them…"

CHAPTER 16

COLLEGE

I must say, I have never experienced much stress in my experience teaching college students. I had one set of evaluations return to me one term where one of the students had given me poor reviews and s/he must have been the one who put the comment "has an obvious bias when it comes to unions." And I recall one term where a student who was a new immigrant to Canada and not quite fluent in the English language argued with me at a break over her low mark on an assignment which was full of spelling and grammatical mistakes. I was generous with the mark I gave her but she insisted it was not fair because she did not have Spellcheck or Microsoft Word at her home. It did not seem like she liked me as a teacher that was for sure, but she passed the course and sent me a thank-you-letter.

When I transferred from teaching gr.7/8 to high school, I knew immediately that for me there was no going back. I knew that if I was transferred back to 7/8, I would probably resign; that I would not survive otherwise (though with affirmations by my side, I could). I won't be transferred to 7/8 because that is not what I am affirming or seeking. And then when I was hired at Algonquin College, I experienced a similar feeling. To me, teaching college was even more fun and less stressful than teaching high school. Now suddenly, I had students that didn't skip class, didn't neglect their homework, and there were no lost textbooks to deal with or irate parents to call back. And the student appraisals were more authentic, though college students also use ratemyprofessor.com. Behavior problems in college are far less frequent than high school and you have behavior management issues in a college classroom they could quickly be solved with affirmations. Not to mention you have the luxury of calling a break or calling security in extreme cases. And in the college system there is far more accountability for extreme behavior issues like threats against a teacher, albeit through a due-process that may seem to be lengthy. However, there are more and more students appealing grades in colleges and universities- it just means one more thing to design an affirmation for.

Typically, appeals may lead to a college instructor losing their patience. They get frustrated when dealing what they perceive as incompetent students, especially those with attitude issues and complete disrespect for authority. This almost always happens at the end of a semester. And most college instructors can't wait for it to be over -it's such a stressful time. During appeal meetings, they have to sit and listen to a student describe how unsupportive and unfair they are as a teacher. And the instructor is tempted to insult back in a politically correct or politically incorrect way since they tend to be wittingly superior, and can do this while faking a caring, supportive voice, so it always works nicely in appeal meetings, usually the professor wins the appeal. This is where the idea of networking with others when it comes to affirmation based pedagogy is important. Sometimes, we are not aware of our actions when we could be. This can be a good thing or a bad thing. You may go into a book store and read an entire book without buying it but feel there is nothing unethical about it since you bought a coffee or two while reading it. But the book store, the publisher, and the author might not condone you doing so.

CHAPTER 17

LUCK

"...in a world easier for dreaming where the most you can do is spend all your time giving some of your time meaning."
–Gord Downie, "Sailboat"

I live in the second coldest capital city in the world, Ottawa. When I was a child, my family decided to go to Florida for Christmas. This was 1983, and as it turned out, that was a record-breaking cold-snap for Florida. We have pictures of me in Florida with my winter coat on. I have been to the Sunshine State many times since but only one time did I go again on Christmas Break. This time it was 2010. And it was even colder than when I was there in '83! As some would say, "just my luck." Let's talk about luck and the school/work place. Paper jams, photo-copier #1 not working, photo copier #2 out of paper, upstairs photo-copier has a line-up, computers not letting you and only you log in, TV/VCR remote is missing batteries, the overhead bulb is burned out, the portable AC is not working and the class clearly stinks, you have no pens. Stop the madness! Change your luck. It's not easy if you happen to have coincidence misfortune syndrome, i.e., a pattern of bad luck because you consider yourself more unlucky than lucky.

Consider this random scenario for a moment: Picture it, downtown Toronto, you need to find a parking spot, there is a parking lot but it will cost $9. You see one spot at a meter, you go for it, you make it, you park. Ah, relief. You then realize you have only $20 bills and one nickel. This one nickel gives you 2 minutes. You go across to a bake store where a nice man who manages the shop is happy to greet you. You order a water bottle, it costs $1.00 and so you then give him your $20. He looks at you and asks, "Do you have anything smaller?" You go through the motions as if looking to see and say 'Sorry.' He checks the till and tells you he has no change. You say 'Thanks anyways' and begin to walk away but before you leave he calls you back and politely says, "Here, take the water." Now you don't want to say "No". You take the water that you didn't want in the first place and leave knowing your 2 minutes has now expired. You go to the next closest store to your spot and buy a lotto ticket for $4. With your change you now have a loonie but afterwards feel bad about the guy in the first store and go in and give him the dollar restoring his faith in humanity, you go back buy another lotto ticket, go back to your meter and put in a dollar. For those of you like me not big on math, you have now spent $8 on lotto tickets, $1 on water you didn't want, and $1.05 on the meter for a total of $10.05 just so you wouldn't have to pay $9 in the parking lot. I can't tell you how many times in my life I have experienced this type of event. For example, I can't even begin to count how many times I have gotten lost while driving or how many times after I got lost I told myself I was going to buy a GPS but held off because I did not have any near future plans of going on a road trip only to get lost horribly the very next day trying to find a place. Would the following situation ever happen to you? Your gas light is on and you are desperately hoping you come to a gas station before you are out of gas! You come to one and there is a car at every pump except one which you pull up to only to realize that there is a bag over the nozzle indicating that it is out of order. You park to the side and wait for what seems like an eternity, nobody who was pumping their gas returns to their car, any sane person would move on and wait 'till the next gas station but your gas light is on remember? Another car pulls in and then another, they now seem to have a better spot to get at one of the pumps when one becomes available. You finally get to a pump and fill up and it is when you go inside that you realize it's one of those gas station/convenience stores with only one employee. You just have to hand him a $20 bill but you will have to wait in what seems like a grocery line for a few minutes before you can go on your way. And then when you exit to your car almost all the pumps are vacant with no cars coming to use them.

Coincidence? Luck? Do you complain to yourself? Dr. Deepak Chopra has illustrated that not only are everyday coincidences meaningful, they actually provide us with glimpses of the field of infinite possibilities that lies at the heart of all things. By gaining access to this wellspring of creation, we can literally rewrite our destinies in any way we wish. "Coincidences" can then be recognized as containing precious clues about particular facets of our lives that require our attention. As you become more aware of coincidences and their meanings, you begin to connect more and more with the underlying field of infinite possibilities. Connect with the filed of infinite possibilities? Now, that sounds exciting.

Have you ever opened the freezer, grabbed the ice-tray, turned it over and water spills all over the place because the ice hasn't frozen yet!? How were you to know, right?! Check off which of these you have experienced or which apply to you:

-has unbelievable bad luck

-Chronic bad hair days

-Forgets to put deodorant on

-Misses the bus, train, plane or gets on the wrong bus, train, or plane

-Paperjam on the printer or photo-copier/pen won't write and no matter how many pens are bought they all get lost

-Flu despite flu shot and if there's a cold going around they are most certainly going to succumb to it

-fan/spectator that always gets hit by the astray tennis ball (or volleyball, whatever)

-the one who spills the drink or gets a drink spilled on them

-Loss of thousands of dollars in their lifetime lending things they never get back and buying things that don't work or break soon after purchase

- During a long drive, efforts to find a good song on the radio are futile and then as s/he pulls into their driveway a great tune comes on, D'oh!

- He goes to the bathroom and zips up right away only to see a very noticeable pee stain on their crotch

-S/he learns to make a checklist before leaving the house on a trip but still always forgets something(s)

- Anything that requires inserting coins (vending, car wash, video game, etc) doesn't work but never an "Out of Order" sign so the money is always lost. They usually respond by putting in more coinage thinking that the first attempt was just a fluke. (As opposed to a friend you have you consider lucky that would look in the slot first and see there was a jam and see several coins backed up inside the slot of earlier unlucky people, and s/he would unwind a paper-clip and fetch out the money)

-wind shield wipers freeze, the wind-shield fluid freezes even though it's anti-freeze

-Winter snow tires removed in spring-like weather in late March and then the next day the most massive snow storm of the year with freezing rain after that

-When s/he goes to get something like their keys out of their pocket, they always, always, always reach into the wrong pocket

- S/he can only carry one small item at a time in any situation, otherwise everything falls, and if it's breakable in any way, it breaks (pretty well everything is breakable, for example, their floss and the whole little contraption breaks into un-repairable bits and pieces)

-While some people will be driving behind a truck and a pebble flings and hits the windshield causing a crack, you may be driving along and out of the blue sky a pebble hits the windshield, causing a crack and that crack of course expands

- S/he stays at a hotel and the room across from them has partying teenagers that are loud and rowdy all night long

-Traffic lights stay red for half a day when you're late

TicketMaster's system offers us our theory in action in a nutshell. When an event goes on sale a "lucky" person wakes up, calls TicketMaster and gets great seats, a less lucky individual will wait in line all night in the cold and then get 300 level seats OR will order them on the Internet and instead of checking the option to have the tickets mailed, they will check the option to pick them up at a TicketMaster Centre. A month later and a day before the event, they will drive twenty minutes to the nearest TM Centre and a couple blocks away realize they have forgotten either the credit card they used to purchase the tickets or ID (both of which are needed to pick up tickets). Why did that thought not cross their minds at some point between leaving the house and the first few minutes of driving en route to? There's a whole litany of other examples. All people experience these things and of course sometimes you can smell the horrendously crappy day on the way, but for unlucky people a "bad day" is a way of life. And it need not be. There's lots of strategies to change your luck. Without a change in consciousness though, it will be a long battle. Simply reading self help books does little. I tried that for years. The #1 bestseller *Don't Sweat the Small Stuff… And it's All Small Stuff* has a lot of great philosophy on how to remove the stress from one's life.... However, saying that it is all small stuff is misleading.

But you know, there's a Norm MacDonald line from *Dirty Work* "Note to self, no matter how bad life gets, there's always beer." Ah yes, optimism is a powerful thing and all's it requires is persistence and B-12 compound pills.... And of course.... the beer..... Though, sadly, some teachers are alcoholics or recovering alcoholics. Worse, many are on anti-depressants.

There's also a scene in the film *Pure Luck* where the character played by Martin Short has chronic bad luck and an experiment is set up whereby a dozen identical chairs are placed in a room and one of them is rigged to fall apart if sat on. He has no idea that this is a test. He is asked to have a seat. He sits on the broken chair and falls.

Perhaps this all can be best illustrated with wasps and bees. Some people are paranoid of bees, wasps, hornets, and the like. These are the ones that always seemed to be swarmed by bees as if a personal attack and they often will be driving along and hear the dreaded sound of the mighty bumble bee in the car. They should never leave their windows down! 'Normal' people don't have a problem at all, they can just chill and let the bees buzz right on by. They say "why do you swat and run? You will only aggravate the bee(s)."

Of course insects don't have brains they can't conceptualize frustration. But speaking of scientific fact, some people have theremones that attract bees more so than others. Well of course! Just as it is in the bee's nature to sting, it is in this person's nature to look foolish in certain situations. But don't fret this does not need be so. It's like genetics. Thinking that your past bad luck renders you generally unlucky for the rest of your life is no different than thinking that your father had kidney stones so you will have kidney stones. You may very well if that's what you think. Just as the scene in *Summer Rental* where John Candy's character's family are waiting in a long long line at a restaurant to be seated and see "VIPs" walking in through ahead of the line and by the time they get to the front of the line it's a twenty minute wait and there's no more lobster, shows that you are not alone. When you're having "one of those days" accept the fact that it may get worse before it gets better and embrace the fact that everyone can relate to your situation. Never give into your frustration. It is just a thought process that can be changed and "luck" can change in seconds. For better or worse. If you are into thinking in terms of probability and think that the odds say that you won't be lucky so why bother trying, remember this: Donna Goeppert of Pennsylvania won a state lotto jackpot not once but twice. 419 million to one were the odds of that happening but odds are irrelevant if you are using affirmations and are mindful. I never understood the quote "Lotteries are a tax on the foolish" since someone has to win the lottery.

Examples of isolated bad luck situations: if you are at a beach and you're watching a beach volleyball game, and the ball hits you in the head; paper-jam, bad hair-day, zit, canker, bomb an exam, runny nose at the wrong place at the wrong time when you have no access to Kleenex, spill beer on yourself or someone, waking up too tired to be fashionably sensitive and you end up looking unfortunate.

Eckart Tolle's pain body theory implies that not only are some people prone to bad luck but so too buildings and places like towns and nations. I grew up in Smiths Falls, Ontario, a rough town with a history of coming up on hard times comparable to Flint, Michigan, but I went to high school in Perth, Ontario, fifteen minutes west, and that town was nothing like Smiths Falls. No offense to my hometown, my heart is dear to it as it so it should but from Chernobyl to Bikini Island, there are places where it may be harder to live, work, raise children, but it can be done and that is the point. It is probably not a coincidence that one of my favorite bands of all time is Bon Jovi. Jon

Bon Jovi grew up in a New Jersey town similar town to mine and some of his biggest songs have had affirmation choruses like *Livin' On A Prayer* or better yet, *Have A Nice Day:*

> Ohhh, if there's one thing I hang onto,
>
> That gets me through the night.
>
> I ain't gonna do what I don't want to,
>
> I'm gonna live my life.
>
> Shining like a diamond, rolling with the dice,
>
> Standing on the ledge, I show the wind how to fly.
>
> When the world gets in my face,
>
> I say, Have A Nice Day.

We begin to form behavioral patterns right from birth. In *Being Happy* Andrew Matthews reveals that the world is a reflection of ourselves. When we hate ourselves, we hate everybody else. Or at least we have little patience for anyone else. I have so many co-workers who you would never be able to tell that they ever get stressed because they always have a smile on their face. I aspire to be like that despite my pain body. When we love being who we are, the rest of the world is wonderful. Matthews goes on to illustrate that there is evidence to suggest that people who have car accidents are often feeling badly about themselves at the time- the accident is partly a subconscious punishment. If there are alternative universes out there, I'm sure I must have died in car accidents!

I let my IDC4O Mindful Healthy Living class listen to the audio of Deepak Chopra's *7 Spiritual Laws* and it echoes all of this business of loving one's self and becoming immune from criticism. It is worth a read or a listen, though I am still not at a point where I can meditate a minimum of one hour a day as he suggests but there is also an even more practical book that he has that I encourage you to read called *The Spontaneous FulFillment of Desire.* He does write about an important point i.e., "Beyond your physical self, beyond your thoughts and emotions, there lies a realm within you that is pure potential." All of us have the capacity to limit the amount of poor luck we experience to the minimum amount destined to us. And the rest can be considered bad coincidences that we set ourselves up for. "…coincidence is involved in guiding and shaping our lives." Every coincidence is a message. And the book proves that being stressed is the worst thing not only in terms of health but in terms of luck and not being able to progress in life. Ah yes, I'd rather have a stress-free life than win the lottery when you think about it, and we all know which one is easier to attain!

There's this one episode of *Seinfeld* where George Castanza is at a car dealership and tries to insert a $1 bill into the snack machine and it keeps ejecting it. Someone else goes and it accepts their bill no problem. Later, George uses change and the Twix bar he seeks starts to unwind out but gets stuck. Now if this has never happened to you it's hard to imagine if it has happened to you, you deserve the same sympathy that all people are entitled to. *Seinfeld* is full of examples where George illustrates bad luck and Jerry good luck. I once lived in an apartment where the one elevator was extremely slow. And I noticed that whenever I entered the building the elevator was never on the ground floor. I adopted a routine whereby I would press the elevator button, walk over to the mail area and check my mail and by the time I would return to the elevator it would be at the lobby ready to take me up to my floor. On any occasion where I was expecting something that day in the mail, the elevator would be at the ground level! So I began using the stairs daily instead, which I should do anyways for the sake of my health but I found that every so often, I would get out of the stairwell on the wrong floor and walk to the wrong apartment that was in the same spot as mine but on a different floor! Certainly, I can see how people use the term luck but I have found that every time I use the stairs correctly, every time the elevator is in the lobby ready for me, every time I remember my cell phone, laptop, keys, etc., I remind myself to be thankful that I have been mindful and it has greatly reduced my so-called bad luck.

Of course there is no doubt that George from *Seinfeld is* well aware that he is prone to bad luck. There was the time he stopped having sex temporarily and became smart (temporarily) and says, "… there was a good chance I was never going to have sex again anyway." When making light of our bad luck it is important to make light of bad luck stories of the past which can provide a good laugh but joking sarcastically about present and future similar luck can be quite counter-productive. Something as small as saying, "I'm such a klutz" actually does reinforce that reality. If I could remove all the times in my life I said to myself, "I'm such an idiot!" I can only imagine the so-called bad luck I would have been spared! But I can't change the past and I can't say "I can change the past" because time travel is not an option but I can change the way I look at the past. This is even more valuable than a time machine would be. I like the old expression about spilled milk. If you keep dwelling about something from the past, you fail to realize that any regret from our past is spilled milk which we learn at a young age is not worth crying over in fact it is worth laughing over. If we spill milk on the floor we should not curse but think "Gee, I'm so glad that spilled on the floor where it is easy to clean and not on my couch." And so what if it was to spill on the couch? It could still be cleaned!

As a professional, you really ought to be lucky more often than not. Our intuition is a key factor and it betrays us once and a while but much less often the so-called lucky person. In the best seller, *Blink*, Malcolm Gladwell does an excellent job illustrating how when we make gut feeling decisions we are "really vulnerable to being guided by our stereotypes and prejudices, even the ones we may not necessarily endorse or believe." So if we are prone to bad luck we are more likely to be less professional.

Suffice to say, that I could write a whole book on luck. And many books have been written on luck. It's really an amazing thing. I have found that overcoming bad luck requires follow through, and not just affirmations. Before I realized this, I had so much bad luck that it's safe to say that I had more bad luck than the average person. For example.... Well... Let's see... I could tell you about....hmmmm...... I could tell you about the time I was taking a train from Ottawa to Niagara Falls and everything that could go wrong did go wrong; the train never made it to Niagara Falls and when we finally did arrive, the taxi brought us and dropped us off at the wrong hotel even though we gave him the exact address. Not something you would expect to happen. How about the time my wife (girlfriend at the time) and I planned to go vacation in Lake George and the first night hotel reservation was for Monday but we had it in our heads that we were not expected there 'till Tuesday. And it was late afternoon when I realized and we made the executive decision to just jump in the car and drive there, late as we would be (come to think of it, it was incredibly lucky that my old Caviler at the time didn't break down on that trip). On the way there, we drove through torrential downpours. Also, we were determined on not getting lost and we would high-five each time we made a correct turn (I did not have a GPS since the cigarette lighter did not work in the Caviler (now, I do have a GPS and I consider it one of the greatest inventions of all time)). Of course, there was the time I drove to Scotia Bank Place to pick up my wife (fiancé at the time) and her daughter after a Justin Bieber concert and though I was there early, I was the last to leave because we could not find each other. It was a debacle. And you simply would not believe how many times I have gotten back from the grocery store and found some products past their expiry date. I am sure you can relate to getting your order messed up at a fast food location but the vast majority of you could not relate to having it happen on an at least a monthly basis (you could say it serves me right for not eating healthy, and you would be right). The last watch I bought had a broken strap when I opened it from the packaging. These things happen. They can happen less often and we can find the humor in them via affirmation mind sets that are based on positivity. Speaking of my old Caviler, when it broke down on me and I had to buy a new car, it hadn't been a week before the low tire light came on the new car; the driver's side tire was going flat! It's comical. I choose to find the humor in it.

Joyce Chapman in *The Live Your Dream Workbook* tells us that "The simple truth is that we participate either knowingly or unknowingly in the process of getting where we are. The more we observe that and pay attention, the more aware we become. It is easier to pretend that we are powerless over the direction our lives are taking- that we are helpless victims- than to accept the truth that we are in control of our own experience. Yet, it is assuming accountability that gives us power over our lives."

No matter how much bad luck bombards you, trust me, the best thing you can do is say: "All is well. Everything is working out for my highest good. Only good will come out of this." (Louise Hay affirmation)

For more ideas on how to deter "bad luck" read *How to Make Luck* by Marc Myers.

I leave you this chapter with a brilliant quote from a song that sums it up by reminding us that without mindfulness (un-mindfulness) when one thing goes wrong it usually leads to another and before long the center does not hold.

"Like boots or hearts or when they start they really fall apart"
-The Tragically Hip-

CHAPTER 18

LEARNING FROM OUR RELATIONSHIPS

Let's talk about relationships. Dr. Oz once said that you need to have at least one hug a day and hold hands at least once a week because among other reasons, affection lowers stress levels. The previous chapter ended with a Tragically Hip quote that was comparing hearts to boots in that once boots have served their purpose they eventually begin to fall apart. When a heart begins to break, there is a lot of heartache on the horizon. The problem can be as simple as people falling in love and for some strange reason thinking that everything will always be domestic bliss. Or, more to the point of this book, teachers making the mistake of assuming that everything will be hunky-dory all semester based on the first day or week of school going so well.

In *The Power* we learn, "A relationship can be on a happy, joyful, exciting, satisfying, and every good feeling frequency. A relationship can also be on a boring, frustrating, worrisome, resentful, depressing, and every bad feeling frequency." Just because it starts out one way does not guarantee that it will always be so. This may be because we have a false sense that if it's good now, it always will be and I don't have to do anything or it may be because based on past experiences, we have it in our assumptions that at some point things will fall apart. It makes me think of words we always spell incorrectly. Some of you are English teachers who literally never make spelling mistakes and you are confident of this ability, most of you though can relate to me when I talk about there being some words that we know, or think we know, that we always spell wrong. I had a friend that always spelled 'their' when he meant 'there' and vice-versa and he knew it. Sometimes, I will be writing a word and think, I'm going to spell this word wrong because I always spell it that way. And sure enough I do. I spelled the word 'acquaintance' incorrectly so many times that just now while I was typing, the automatic spell-check corrected it for me. You do not have to a brain expert to know that our brains are good at learning but also good at solidifying habits.

As every union can tell you, we really need to be more mindful when it comes to our relationships with our co-workers. Having said that, however, I believe it is a fine idea to go without having contact with your co-workers on your summer vacation. Two months is never enough time to do everything you want to on holidays and seeing co-workers will often take a back-seat, though with time, positive affirmations will make you more successful at accomplishing your summer goals. During the school-year though you should go about getting along with your co-workers the same you would friends, family, and significant others knowing that becoming unforgiving, unsympathetic, or intolerant will beget more and more animosity and more and more break-downs in communication. You don't always have to be in the staff room and you don't always have to avoid the staff room.

Michael Losier has recently come up with a helpful concept called "future pacing" (a way to communicate to another person that whatever s/he may have been anticipating as a negative experience or outcome could very well turn out to be a positive one). I think using future pacing is a great strategy to use with co-workers and students. It makes everyone more optimistic. Students will be less resistant. On episode 2 of *Shark Tank* there was a teacher who started a business based on getting students more interested in English by among other things, recording a CD with songs about Shakespearian plays ("Classroom Shakespeare Session Jam"). His positive attitude, and his creativity as well as his future pacing (getting the students to see value in learning the content) are all connected. Teachers can talk to parents about future pacing at parent interviews when the topic of homework assignments is being addressed.

I have a sister who is a college instructor in social work and is a reiki master. She has a screen-saver with the quote "When the student is ready the teacher appears." That teacher is Mom or Dad for millions of students. I've taught students who were home-schooled and if you are a parent home-schooling your child, you ought to consider zeroing-in on social interaction affirmations with your child. Social interaction is critical to getting ahead in life.

You may be married to someone who is not a teacher and who does not like their job and their complaining gets in the way of your positive affirmations. Share with them that job success and affirmations in general can improve anyone's outlook on their job. Louise Hay says: "I'm a great believer in blessing every person, place, and thing in the workplace with love." She believes that the environment you work in will respond in kind. The opposite of this is complaining about your job or co-workers. She suggests writing or typing the following affirmation and putting it where you can see it at work every day: "My job is a peaceful haven. I bless my job with love. I put love in every corner, and my job lovingly responds with warmth and comfort. I am at peace."

Sometimes getting along with a student, co-worker, administrator, or loved one can seem impossible. At times like this, I am reminded of the quote: "Aerodynamically, a bumble bee shouldn't be able to fly. But it doesn't know that." Anything is possible.

Try these work relationship affirmations I have recently designed:

-It's exciting working with great co-workers

-I'm glad none of my co-workers who come from all walks of life, are not boring

-I am happy that some of my co-workers are good friends too

-I trust all my colleagues

-I feel ecstatic knowing how supportive my friends and acquaintances at work are

-I feel passionate about my work just as my colleagues do

-I feel blissful about the morale in my workplace

-I truly respect and look up to my co-workers

Remember this too, in life, when we go through our most depressing or traumatic experiences which we have, and will, our relationships can be the swing-vote in whether or not we hit or avoid "rock bottom." If we have abundant support from our relationships then it is because we are attracting support. I have been to the mouth of Hell at "rock bottom" and back twice in my life where I knew I was literally depressed, but I bounced back much quicker the second time thanks to the support of my loving wife, therefore, truer words were never spoken when *The Power* states: "If something negative has happened in your life, you can change it. It is never too late, because you can always change the way you feel."

When I look back on my career and I can think of many instances where I was offended by a student or co-worker and I dwelled on it. And I can feel the stress associated with that mind-set. Like any relationship, when we dwell on a negative aspect we feel sick. The affect our intentions have here in any type of relationship are counter-productive. I have been guilty of sending harmful intentions to people. If we want to be happy and successful we have to forgive our lover, family, friends, co-workers, students, parents, administrators, government, corporations and strangers. Perhaps it has to start with strangers and work its way up. When you judge anyone of these, ask yourself, how would you like it if you were being judged by them? The stranger on the motorcycle driving by my house with an unbearably loud muffler might be a great husband and father despite my initial reflex thought that he is an inconsiderate jerk. Dr. David R. Hamilton concludes: " ... what you give out always comes back to you in one form or another. Being genuinely good to people is a good way to improve your overall health..." And he goes on to make reference to Patch Adams who dedicated his life to saving and enhancing lives on the premise that laughter is the best medicine. I love to laugh. If you do to but know that you laugh less often now then you did when you were in your twenties, you ought to find ways to laugh more often. Try going to Yuk Yuk's or browse the humor section of any book store. But humor should not be the only focus since happiness more so than humor in and of itself is the best medicine. Therefore, always visit the self-help/well-being and metaphysical section of the bookstore too. Check out the recommending readings I have listed at the end of this book.

CHAPTER 19

PARTICIPATION

Every teacher knows that the ideal classroom has students who participate in the class. The opposite tends to happen more often, i.e., the classroom with blank stares, students sleeping, no questions being asked or answered and so on. Imagine a radio talk-show where there are no callers. Even if there were e-mailer's e-mails being read on air, how long would you listen? The key lies with what Michael Losier calls "Positive Presupposition." I'm delighted to picture myself using this strategy in the classroom. It is so beneficial. Even before I read his work I knew some of the truths spoken of. Many a seasoned teacher already knew these things through trial and error I suppose. In fact, when I was doing my placement, my supervisor pointed out to me that I was wrong to use questions like:

"Does anyone know…?"

"Does anybody have a question?"

"Make sense?"

He told me that these questions won't get answered. The students don't need to answer the question and if they need to ask a question they will be too shy to do so. It seems too simple but rewording these questions slightly leads to amazing results. Reword your questions in a way that implies that you assume someone wants to answer and/or would have the answer. This is what you will be affirming. You will know your class and figure out how to best do this. There may be times where you have the time to go to each student one at a time to elicit a question and/or comment. This is OK. But to elicit the best class discussions have some default questions such as: "Who would like to go first?" (most often someone here will and once you get six people to respond you will get the majority of the group involved and you will have the attention of the whole class).

I've used this one, "I have a gut feeling that there are a couple of you who have questions. Who is that?"

I've also used what my old high school Communications/Technology teacher used to say, "Any questions… comments… snappy remarks…?" This makes the students feel more at ease and I've never once had a student literally make a snappy remark when I say this as if it would be their cue. When the students are talking amongst themselves and it is on topic it is wonderful. These are the moments that our job is the easiest. However, these are the times where sooner or later, 'on topic' transforms into anything but. Gone are the days when you could clap or turn the lights off to get the students refocused though this may still work with most primary classrooms. As I mentioned earlier, I yell "YO!" and my students know to yell "YO!" back in unison and that is followed by silence. It works well (you will find with the odd group that it won't work if there are a couple of students who insist on yelling or talking after the "Yo!" though taking them aside after class and talking to them about that specifically more often than not will work). There are countless other little tricks to use; try different things each year that you haven't tried before. It is an easy job being a teacher when your students are quiet. What an important affirmation. Carol Ann Tomlinson talks about minimizing noise as an important factor in a differentiated classroom, she says, "When students are active in a classroom, there will be some noise. There is no need for noise to become oppressive or distracting. From the beginning of the year, work with students on working with peers quietly. Teach them to whisper or talk softly…" If you have a student that can't work when the noise level is high even when it is an acceptable on-task noise level, offer that student ear plugs, this will usually work as long as you don't wear ear plugs in the class, the optics on that would be grounds for concern. There are more classroom management resources now than ever before for teachers thanks to the Internet and Facebook (there are many teacher Facebook groups).

I never understood why so many administrators speak against using humor in the classroom. It is absolutely true that humor deters bad behavior. Yet I know of no teacher who uses humor in their lesson plan when being observed by their principal. Maybe the principal figures that when using humor the students can get too far side-tracked or it can be inappropriate. Sarcasm for example is hard to defend. Though the best teacher I ever had was my high school history teacher who used sarcasm every day in his lessons it was never directed at students though. That's the difference. Why would you want to direct your sarcasm at a student this is the opposite of a positive affirmation. Harmless general sarcasm is fine like when my students are roaring laughing about something and I say, "OK, let's get cereal." They laugh at the play-on words (when said aloud, it sounds similar to "let's get serious"). But they always quiet down and listen and move on at that point. Don't be afraid to use humor even when you are being appraised. Yes, there are some administrators who are anal-retentive. I had one co-worker who when appraised was docked for using nicknames with students. Know your administrator. Appropriate classroom shtick is what the students want and it need not be inappropriate. Teachers know what is and what is not appropriate. With the use of positive affirmations you will be more conscious of this.

If you are a consultant at a school board and you are thinking that this book will mislead teachers into thinking that all they have to do is positive affirmations and not worry about other professional development like workshops on numeracy, differentiated instruction, brain research, literacy strategies, media or business literacy symposiums (etc), let me be clear, the more PD the better. Over the last few years, I have attended many workshops on critical literacy at my school board and while not all of them were interesting or beneficial for me, most were. Through them, I have developed a clear understanding of what critical literacy is. And I believe that it has greatly helped me as an English teacher but I think that good PD transcends subject matter; all teachers need to focus on creating contexts that promote critical literacy. I recommend the book that the Curriculum Department in my board gave me: *Critical Literacy- Enhancing Students Comprehension of Text* by Maureen McLaughlin and Glenn L Devoogd through Scholastic. How many times have teachers heard over and over that we need to know what kind of learners our students are? I don't even know if I am visual, auditory, or kinesthetic let alone my students and the easiest way to scrutinize a teacher is to say they do not have a balance of visual, auditory, and kinesthetic lesson plan delivery. It helps to affirm that you realize that the more you know about how each style likes to learn, the better able you will be to connect with your students. We need schools where the majority of teachers connect with the majority of their students. As much as I clearly indicated that I have little respect for Ratemyteacher.com, it is apparent that one thing all schools have in common is that there are only two or three teachers at each school that get top ratings. This tells me that only a couple of teachers are able to connect with the majority of their students in a meaningful way. Losier says of teaching techniques that stimulate each style, "Understanding the way each style prefers to receive and process information will allow you to design and employ a variety of teaching techniques that will accommodate and appeal to all types of students." You will also in turn be able to tell parents at parent-night what type of learner their child is and how low-and- behold, you are implementing strategies to accommodate this. Furthermore, the "Master Teacher" Vol.34 Number 14: "Eight Ways to Create A Productive Climate" talks about eight strategies which we can incorporate into our affirmations.

1) A high profile as an advocate is vital (Students need to believe you care about them and you are an advocate for them)

2) You must be fair and not have favorites. (We all do have favorites. I have run into many students after I was done teaching them and some I remembered their name because I so enjoyed teaching them, others I remembered their name because I truly hated having them in my class and others I didn't know their name and didn't remember ever teaching them).

3) Attack problems not people.

4) Positive attitude

5) Focus on the future not the past (repeat this to yourself many times)

6) Empower students; share power

7) Show character (to me, this means being assertive and having a super personality. And I think having a differentiated classroom comes into play here as well. Carol Ann Tomlinson has stated, "Teachers construct differentiated classrooms in varying ways depending on their own personalities, the nature of the subject and grade level they teach, and the learning profiles of their students.")

8) Be cheerful, friendly, and enthusiastic: "The master teacher knows the goal of high productivity and high satisfaction for everyone- student and teacher alike- is a tenet of education. Unless we're aiming for this climate goal, it's almost impossible to get high productivity and high satisfaction for students- or for ourselves." And in terms of motivation, "The Master Teacher" puts it well: "Making negative generalizations about the school can affect students- and your efforts to motivate students in your class. For instance, you should never make such comments as "This place is so disorganized" or "You can't get anything done here" or "How can I teach with all the interruptions?" I remember at one point the classes were getting interrupted at my school several times a period needlessly, it was ridiculous. Even the students were getting agitated and I knew it was impeding on my lessons. It was so annoying that classes were being interrupted to page a student to the office who could have just as easily be summoned by his/her class being called directly. And some teachers were constantly complaining about it. Some teachers couldn't care less and were annoyed that other teachers were complaining about (I always wondered what they were doing in their class that they were oblivious to the interruptions). I met with the secretary and the principal and we discussed this issue in a friendly way and the interruptions were reduced by about seventy-five percent. I was pleased. Most teachers were pleased. Of course this meant I couldn't page "All student council members report to the Student Council meeting in portable 6" which meant that I never had 100% attendance of council members at my meetings. But it was an acceptable sacrifice.

CHAPTER 20

THE UNION (AS A PROFESSIONAL ASSOCIATION)

Let's talk about the union as a professional association. First of all, I am amazed that so many people in North America are not in a union. I am amazed that there are teachers who are anti-union. I am amazed that there are teachers teaching in private schools that are not in unions. I am saddened that the Colleges in Ontario do not allow their part-time instructors to unionize even though it would be in everyone's best interest if they did and the part-time instructors have made it clear through a vote two years ago that they wanted to unionize. Did you know that in Sweden, if you work at McDonald's, you are in a union? Unions have led to countless job enhancements and opportunities because they began with such noble and positive passions. As we know though, so often union-staff are bogged-down with grievances to the point that the union is kept from achieving its full potential in its support to its members. For example, committees can be shelved in lieu of busy workloads. This is why I would urge union leaders to offer workshops to their members on affirmations and mindfulness. I guarantee you that there would be a drop in the rate of grievances and false accusations against teachers. The union in turn, would have more money and time to support its members. One who is anti-union might be tempted to argue that if we were mindful, we would not need a union at all. Perhaps, but if we remember that as teachers our union is more than just a union, it is a driving force behind professional development, social justice, political action, and support resources for all its members and their families. It is a professional association.

I would urge all teachers to resist the temptation to be anti-union. So often, I hear teachers complain about their union dues when in reality, I bet that they would still be complaining about the union if it were free. The union helps members in need constantly. What goes up must come down and what goes out must come back. Unions can reap the benefits of helping others. Some teacher unions need to do a better job of course that goes without saying. Be mindful that most teacher unions offer hardship grants, workshops, PD funding, conferences, lobbying the government on your behalf (etc.). Like any union, it needs to be respected since it is an organization of workers who have banded together to achieve common goals in key areas and working conditions. The negotiation of wages alone is undeniable. Teachers would make far less if they weren't or aren't in a union with the exception of a few private schools (most private schools in fact pay far less and even the ones that do not usually do not have benefits or retirement packages that compare to the unionized system). The union strives to promote legislation favorable to the interests of their members as a whole. To this end, they may pursue campaigns, undertake lobbying, or financially support individual candidates or parties. The union does a lot of good and would do more good with more support of its members.

School boards and unions can work together with joint PD committees and talk about building character and better behavior in students via mindfulness based pedagogy.

Unions have the hardest job when it comes to mindfulness though. I mean they really have their work cut out for them given the nature of the line of work. When the union meets with the members, what are the questions and answers being discussing? Most of the time, they have to do with problems, injustices, arguments, and accusations. When the union's PD committee, political action committee, or staffing committee sit down to meet, what must the starting point be? What's wrong and what's not working? What is the board doing that they're not supposed to be doing? After all, most of the suggestions to the board from the union that come out of these committees/meetings come about based on surveys that reflect what teachers are disgruntled about. And the union president has a harder job than any principal because they have to respond almost daily to teachers who are in crisis. The teacher in crisis as an individual, and the union as a whole, can easily lose sight that they can bog themselves down. Sure, they can file their thirty grievances a year, but the board knows at the end of the day, they don't have to do anything the union says. The board's priority is to make sure they are following legislation thereby ensuring that the government of the day isn't issuing suggestions or orders to them. Although, if the government was to find out that a board was not fulfilling expectations of a certain bill it was probably the union that made the board aware of this in the first place and perhaps the union that eventually let the government know. *The Power* teaches how to be mindful when dealing with negative situations applicable to individuals or groups who have no choice but to react to a bad situation. It warns that we have to be very careful because we tend to "react with negative feelings to something that has happened." This in turn gives out negative vibes thereby attracting more negative vibes. "They become trapped in a cycle by their own feelings. Their life goes around and around in circles not getting anywhere, like a hamster on a wheel, because they don't realize that to change their life, they must change their feeling frequency!" The union has to avoid viewing board administration as anti-union. Of course some of them are just as some teachers are. What good will come out of dwelling on this? If it is to ever change, it will be because of a shift in consciousness on the part of the union. Then, and only then, will the boards get along better with the unions. An example of one small thing teachers can do to foster this is whenever we first hear of a new board policy that seems "out- to- get" the teacher, we should first take a mindful approach and say, "I don't have the board's side of the story yet. What could it be? Is there a pro-teacher reasoning that I can imagine that they may be thinking? If your first reaction is, "here they go again, making our jobs harder and setting us up for more work and stress", there is only negative affirmations. Unless the board is proposing a pay cut, their heart is probably in the right place even if we disagree.

As a History major, I strongly believe that those who do not learn from history are condemned to repeat it and if we are not mindful then we are incapable of learning the lessons history offers. When it comes to the union, again, they have their work cut out for them in this regard since it can't be helped to talk about the past. It can be very important for new teachers, for example, to learn about situations in the past that need to be avoided at all costs. In the province of Ontario for example, the union has an obligation to never forget the vendetta against teachers that former Premiere Mike Harris had, having said that, it is even more important to be positive when looking back and always say things will always be better than that dark period. Otherwise, we look back feelingly of mistakes and regret and we can set ourselves up for what we vowed never to go through again. As I write this, the Conservative Party in Ontario (the party that was in power when Mike Harris was Premiere) has a platform calling for TPAs (Teacher Performance Appraisals) to be public (i.e. any parent would be able to look this information up. I can't imagine if my TPA from 2005 was made public when I had a horrible principal who gave me a very belittling TPA. I disagreed with all the wording in the TPA. It would be wrong if that was made public. Simply wrong. Also, this group of politicians are calling for bonuses for teachers based on performance, and for cuts to education, and worse of all, this party has it in their minds that Kindergarten teachers are overpaid and overrated and they should be replaced by early childhood educators who teach daycare. The Conservative Party is not very mindful and they should at least be more mindful when it comes to education given that when Harris was in power it led to a province- wide strike of political action. I have to put my money where my mouth is though here and say that even in the event of a Conservative victory next year, the teaching profession will continue to improve just as it is meant to. I also have to acknowledge that the leaders of this party may very well a) have their heart in the right place and want to better the education system and are not just trying to implement this to get votes and b) are mindful of history and know better than to make the same mistakes Harris did.

I've known teachers that have feared the union because either they fear losing their seniority if they get blacklisted and/or because they fear that someday they may need their union rep. If you need to call your union rep it probably does not mean you are a bad teacher. Most teachers are in fact mindful, just not twenty-four hours a day. Workshops for teachers put on jointly by the boards and the unions will lead to far less teachers needed their union in this capacity and free up the union to be the active professional association it is destined to be.

CHAPTER 21

STRESS

Ah, stress. Imagine a world without it? I always say 99% of the problems in the world are from people not getting along and how much more would people get along if they did not have stress in their lives? How much more energy would you have in the classroom if you didn't have stress in your life?

Have you ever been annoyed because you can't find your keys or cell phone, or name tag, or when you are delayed in traffic or you can't find a parking spot? Have you ever been in a shopping mall during Christmas shopping hours and wanted to run out of the store? If you answered 'no', then I believe you, I've known teachers that to my knowledge, have never come "out of character." I have never seen them get frustrated. And if you answered 'no', you may find you pretty much don't have a lot of stress in your life right now. You should read this chapter anyway as it may come in handy and it will at least help you better relate to those co-workers or students you encounter who are under stress. Some of you will have, however, answered 'yes'. A select few of you perhaps even have experienced deep levels of frustration over these things more times than you care to admit, like myself. Heck, I don't want to tell you how many times I didn't make a lunch for school in the morning because I was too late, too lazy, or didn't have any food in my house and then went to the cafeteria at lunch (I was their best customer), and expressed frustration over their lack of service and lack of selection and of course lack of quality. Do you see the disconnect? I would have no reason to complain about the cafeteria if I brought a lunch. It got to the point where many of my co-workers made fun of how much I was eating cafeteria food. And then when I finally started bringing lunches regularly, and they were healthy enough with fruits and/or veggies, they made fun of me for that too!

I look forward to weekends, as I'm sure you do to, and there's nothing wrong with that, there's meant to be less stress on the weekends, but how many of us enjoy our weekend and then undo it Sunday at 3:00 because we realize we are behind in our marking and/or planning? Stop ruining your weekends! It's unnecessary stress. Actually all stress is. People that live to be 105 year-old have had a life with less stress to show for it than the average person.

When I attended the *I Can Do It* Conference put on by Louise Hay and Hayhouse in Toronto in May 2010, one of the speakers, Maria Shimoff said that stress causes 90% of disease and she listed the top five stressors as:

1. going to work in the morning
2. kids
3. communicating
4. time
5. finances

I can recall many times getting up in the morning not wanting to go to work as I'm sure you can as well. As a teacher I have often dreaded certain students. I have had stressful fights with friends or family that I know was a simple case of communication break-down. I always feel like I do not have enough time to accomplish everything I have to do let alone what I want to do. And I know all too well what it is like to get in financial hot water. Shimoff knows that happiness is the answer and taught us that fifty percent of happiness is genetic (this certainly explains why stress management skills come so much more naturally to others), while forty percent is due to habits and ten percent is that which comes from circumstances (so why do people focus on that ten percent?) Stress is a complicated thing, and we know how wonderful our summer vacation is because we associate it with less stress, which is OK but we have to be careful with those Christmas/Spring Break/ Summer holiday countdowns. We are defying the law of attraction if our thoughts are saying "I will be happy or stress free when I'm on holidays." It is a good idea to be excited and look forward to a vacation and you can do well to visualize the specific smoothness and pleasantness of the holiday but relax and calmly await the actual date of its arrival. Otherwise, you may be inadvertently sabotaging your vacation. The worst thing that can happen in all this is when you experience frustration or anger when you are actually on holidays. Anger leads to suffering because it is the worst form of stress. Buddha said: "Holding on to anger is like grasping a hot coal with the intent of throwing it at someone else; you are the one getting burned."

One Louise Hay affirmation that I wrote down a long time ago in my first ever affirmations journal was: "When there is a problem, I say in repetition: 'All is well. Everything is working out for my highest good. Only good will come out of this.'" I said it daily for 3 years and then it dawned on me that I never actually did this. Here I was saying this and it was useless because I never actually did it. So I really meditated on it and starting doing it and found that I could create a stress free world (at least stress free in comparison to my life up to that point).

Think back to the affirmations chapter (Ch.1) when I talked about my making things worse by focusing on my limitations and fears instead of overcoming them. What an awful dreadful thought to have in the summer that problems at school are just around the corner awaiting you. Dreading the start of the school year is common for the majority of teachers. This gets in the way of us enjoying our summer and it plants seeds of stress that we will later upon its manifestation blame solely on students, co-workers, administrators, and/or parents.

This chapter you are reading right now is probably the most important chapter in the book since you all want to know how to eliminate stress from your life. Several times in this book I point out the importance of a quiet learning environment. A noisy one is stressful for everyone whether you admit that or not. Try saying to the students on the first day that you have two rules, and two rules only, 1) Do not speak out when I am at the front of the class teaching without raising your hand and 2) Act your age. Your school has a handbook or student agenda with school rules that cover all the other bases. Rule #2 is the key rule. Because it doesn't matter how old a student is, if they are being immature they are not acting their age. I knew a teacher who says on the first day, "There are 2 rules: 1) Don't put your feet on the desk and 2) Act your age." So I suppose you can substitute Rule #1 with anything arbitrary. Just pick something that drives you nuts. For me my #1 rule here would still be don't talk out when I am at the front of the class teaching.

In the documentary self-help film *The Shadow Effect*, we learn that "either you use it or it will use you" "it" being your shadow, and your shadow being that part of you that does or seeks harm. Our shadow which we all have otherwise we would not be human, can be a great source of stress especially for teachers. This is even more dangerous when we have a semester where we have an extensive amount of behaviors to deal with.

In such times, we tend to be forgetful of the fact that what we judge in others is a disowned part of oneself. How many times have you heard that when you are pointing a finger at someone, you have 3 pointed back at yourself? Meaning, we hate in others what we hate in ourselves. It is a different type of "hate" when we hate some evil in the world. I don't know what part of myself I hate when I think of Hitler or Bin Laden since I would never kill another person. But the motives of the distain are totally different. One thing is for sure, as illustrated in *The Shadow Effect* is that what you resist, will persist. So think of all the times you have had a student that you had conflicts with and nothing you did could change the student's behavior and think of the stress associated with that. And was it necessary stress?

No amount of positive thinking can make us immune from stress so long as our bodies produce stress hormones. Teaching is a stressful career plain and simple. Many teachers suffer from heart disease, ulcers, obesity, substance abuse, depression, immune system suppression, or are on anti-depressants. There was an article on CNN's website in 2010 saying that meditation and mindfulness are now more effective than anti-depressants. I had a co-worker once explain to me that he was not an alcoholic because his drinking did not interfere with his work. Yet he drank every night and would often drink an entire bottle of wine by himself in one sitting. Stress management can come in one of a thousand ways but unfortunately, only some of them are free of side-effects. Just because you are a high functioning alcoholic, does not mean you aren't one.

Dr. Brian L Weiss wrote in "Eliminating Stress Finding Inner Peace": "Many people are completely oblivious to, or only partially cognizant of, the levels of stress they may be shouldering every day. Many are not aware of the most common causes of stress."

I once told a co-worker that I was very glad to be marrying someone who appreciated how hard teachers work and how stressful a job it is; to which he replied, "It's only as stressful as we make it." This is true of course. Even though it is true, it does not mean that it is not a stressful job. Deadlines in terms of annual learning plans and/or long range plans, report cards, culminating tasks and final exams add up to plenty of reason to stress-out. Young teachers with small children at home often do not get enough sleep and often do not have time to nap. And for the department-heads and administrators, the stress of teachers not meeting those deadlines can be cause for worry. Many of the teachers who neglect deadlines feel that since there are no real consequences for students who hand work in late why should they take deadlines so seriously? This is understandable logic but it is both counter-productive and is clearly a negative affirmation. It is understandable but as my principal has said many times, "We are here for the students first and foremost." That is an important affirmation. A prime directive of an affirmation actually. My principal has said at staff meetings in terms of deadlines, "You got to respect those deadlines gang, after all, we expect our students to hand work in on time."

Brian Weiss ranks frequent deadlines or unhealthy competition at work or at school on the same significant level as losing a loved one or being fired!

So what do you do to combat stress? Of course there are many things you could do. You could exercise, go on vacations, visit spas, get massages, go to comedy clubs, engage in creative writing, pray, sleep in, go to your favorite restaurant, attend rock concerts, amusement parks, PD conferences, sporting events, or you could give to charity (etc). Find what works for you. For me, I love any of these but going to hotels as a retreat is very conducive to meditation. If I am going on a vacation or to a conference I like to select a hotel where I can meditate and relax and feel a sense of freedom. I don't know what it is about hotels but that works for me it might not work for you.

I like roller coasters, you may not, I like thunder storms but you may not. Find what works and always be looking for new ways to deal with stress; the more ways, the better. Perhaps, religious pilgrimages is the order of the day for you. By the way, if you do love hotels as much as I do, may I suggest: the Delta on the 401 in Scarborough, Ontario (outside of Toronto) (get a room with a balcony overlooking the atrium near the pool and have your door open at night and fall asleep to the sound of the waterfall; The Renaissance Marriot SkyDome Hotel inside the Rogers Centre in Toronto (get a suite or a room with a view into the Dome); the Best Western in Gatlinburg, Tennessee (get a room with a balcony overlooking the creek); Embassy Suites in Niagara Falls (get a suite overlooking the falls); Brookstreet Resort in Kanata, Ontario (outside of Ottawa); l'hotel de la Montange in Montreal, Quebec; the Day's Inn in Panama City Beach, Florida (all rooms have a view of the ocean); unique 5-star hotels in Disney World, Las Vegas, or Atlantis can be very a healthy route of healthy escapism as well albeit costly. Let me know if you know of any hotels that are particularly tranquil and peaceful and conducive to meditation and relaxation.

In 2009-10, my school board's theme was "We Walk in Good Company..." This is a reference to Jesus but also to all the saints and angels and fellow Catholics and Christians around us carrying out the call as ambassadors of Christ and beacons of light to spread love and peace. We walk in good company is an affirmation. But it requires that you have an open mind and to practice what you preach.

If we are to walk in good company and be mindful of its message, then we need to model behavior, specifically in this case, to be more Christ-like. In "Messages from Your Angels" by Doreen Virtue, the angels of God call out: "Where you see hopelessness, we always see hope. Where you may see ravaged scars, we always see health. Where you may experience prolonged agony, we always see the way out of pain." They go on to say, "'Learning' is actually 'unlearning', where you forget your ego-established ideas."

This reminds me of how one year my board distributed "WWJD" wrist bands to all the staff and students. It's a great idea. Not everyone wore them and most didn't wear them for the entire year let alone beyond, but those who did were affirming that they sought to be guided by the example of Jesus. This is the opposite of stress when we seek ways to better ourselves and our world.

Having said all that, what is the most important stress reliever? You guessed it by now, positive thinking. But don't be fooled. As I said earlier, we are never immune from stress altogether. So we also need to make sure we are healthy in mind and body.

I believe that if you believe that today's young people lack the attitudes and behaviors that virtually all societies, cultures, and faith traditions value, then you are making a negative affirmation, one that carries with it stress. It's so easy to be a pessimistic prophet of doom. The public perception is that schools are falling apart. Though *Boston Public, Freedom Writers, Dangerous Minds, Lean On Me,* and *The Breakfast Club* are critically acclaimed and rightly so, Hollywood has reinforced this stereotype every time a TV show or movie comes out about teaching. Though at least in the examples I just gave, the script reveals that the parents and the home-life are the primary cause of misbehavior. If all parents gave character training in the home, how easy would it be to be a teacher? Virtually everyone would want to be or be open to be a teacher. I would take a pay-cut if all parents did this. But let's face reality. Decades of talk about character-education has led to little change in schools. When EQAO (provincial testing) results came out in Ontario for 2009, ten of the top eleven schools were Catholic schools. And I remember one caller on a radio talk show weighing in on why this was so- talking about schools with a strong sense of community and identity. He said even the secretaries at the Catholic schools he knew of, referred to the students as 'their kids' as if they were talking about their own children. What if we combine character-education (deliberate attempt to help young people identify, understand, and do the right thing regardless of circumstances) with teaching students to value community and identity and incorporated affirmations? Such a comprehensive program infused into the curriculum and school environment can and will, have a decided effect on the dynamics of a school. Less stress levels would be felt by all.

Affirm that you spend less time disciplining and more time teaching thereby attracting less stress in your job; I promise you that you will have less stress. I would urge schools to put more time into recognizing character and virtuous action. Some schools have ARK programs (A Random Act of Kindness) certificates which are great but they would be more effective if a) more students were given them and b) the recipients were recognized at an assembly. Also, some schools have The Terrific Kid Program which is great but is not taken seriously at many schools since principals in many schools demand that the teacher give each and every student in the class a certificate at least once during the school year.

Earlier I said that 99% of problems are noise-level related. I can't fully understand why so many students speak out in class without raising their hand. But I do know it usually reflects their home life and upbringing. "The Master Teacher" offers this solution: "...use the code of reciprocity. People are more likely to go along with your ideas if you give them something they want- first. Second, call people to nobler conduct. Rather than tell them to stop interrupting, simply ask them to raise their hand and be identified before speaking- without mentioning the interruptive factor." Again, to us, given our upbringing, we would assume that it should be enough to say "Stop disrupting the class." But clearly, little changes in language are like changes in the tone of your voice and I have never known a good teacher that is in the habit of yelling.

Let's talk about the stress that comes from a lack of support from administration. Principals and their vice-principals can peg teachers into one of two categories: those who they never associate behavior problems with and those that do. And guess which of the two get more support? If a student tells me to 'fuck off' (something I have never experienced), s/he may get a one day inside-school-suspension whereas if 'Mr. Perfect Teacher Principal-Want –To- Be' gets told to 'f- off' you can be rest-assured that the student will be suspended for three, maybe four days. Administrators who get into the habit of ignoring and abandoning their teachers who they deem to be on their own because they must be doing something wrong, are doing a great disservice to all parties. They themselves are affirming that they aren't good enough to deal with the conflicts. Principals and vice principals who reinforce bad behavior and allow bullies to flourish are first and foremost to blame for the way bullying is out of hand right now in our schools. However, in mindfulness, blame is irrelevant since it is a negative affirmation that is not healthy and can be unprofessional. Ignoring a bully is rewarding a bully and always dishing out meaningless one day inside school suspensions is another reward because there is no progression and thus, no real consequence. As long as there is no consequence, the behavior will repeat. Here it is affirmed loud and clear, we encourage you to be who you are, bully to your heart's delight.

Sometimes teachers step down from doing extra-curriculars in response to a lack of support. I don't blame them. It is, however, a negative affirmation.

When administrators are not supportive of your classroom learning environment they are not supportive of your focus on the plan and purpose of your career which is a stress-reducing visualization.

Teachers should start a) indicating on their annual learning plans the amount of support they expect from their administration and b) viewing obstacles as learning lessons opportunities. My research shows that this change in viewpoint reduces stress.

In "Messages From Your Angels" it is said, "Wherever you find stress, you will find feelings of victimhood.... All stress is self-imposed, since all stress-inducing situations are elected by your own free will. There are no exceptions..." I don't agree with that last part since as teachers we can never leave the classroom when we are stressed the only thing we can do is remove a student and even that doesn't always work. I once ejected a student from a classroom and he refused to leave and I called the Student Support Worker's phone, no answer, the vice principal's office, no answer, and the principal's office, no answer. Sounds like law of attraction timing, doesn't it?

Let's not forget that gossip in the workplace is an obvious form of stress. Schools are a cesspool of gossip among students but also teachers. In the June 2010 *Psychology Today* magazine, there was an article called: "Solutions- How To Be A Good Gossip" by Emily Anthes. And right off the top, it begins with a story at an elementary school where the staff viewed a new principal as bullying and unsympathetic. They spent a lot of time gossiping about the principal. Gossip is a weapon of the weak and I myself have been very guilty of engaging in it. As a union rep for several years, I thought I did a good job keeping classified information to myself on many occasions meanwhile knowing that it goes with the territory that people will often assume the worse behind your back. The interesting thing about the Anthes article is that it shows that while gossip can ruin peoples lives (which can be a process sped up by social media sites I admit), it can bring co-workers together in a positive way when the gossip shifts from digging up dirt to stating something positive you heard about someone. Over time, this positive form of gossip becomes as satisfying as traditional gossip. It is clearly important that you protect yourself by simply wording everything carefully. And teachers can be very good at this. One study in the article referenced a group of teachers that would imply criticism of their current principal by speaking positively about his/her predecessor.

Stress boils down to one thing: luck. I have always known this. One of the first non-fiction books I ever bought was called "How To Make Luck." Rebecca Webber wrote an article called "Make Your Own Luck: Five Principals For Making The Most of Life's Twists, Turns, and Coincidences." The article is in part based on the book *The Luck Factor* by Richard Wiseman. Here are the five principals:

1) See serendipity everywhere (I think being mindful and teaching mindfulness makes this a lot easier and I think it's the most important factor; your affirmation here should sound something like this: "I am lucky, I attract profound good luck, I see opportunities of growth everywhere),

2) Prime yourself for chance (I think this backs up all of Malcolm Gladwell's work in that we need to refrain from judging people and things by their cover; "Cognitive flexibility can be cultivated..." is how Gladwell puts it. We all need to consider both sides of a story, we teach our students this from gr.1-12 do we not? I know of one school board that had a massive surplus in benefits account but refused to enhance the benefits and the union responded by making a petition and silently protesting at all the board meetings with buttons that said: "Healthy Teachers, Healthy Schools" and the impression that teachers got was that the board had tried to pull the wool over their eyes and restrict access to benefits that teachers had paid for. If you were in that situation, would you jump to the conclusion that the board is conspiring or would you ask, "What is the Board's side of the story?" We should strive to be positive and pro-active and this skill of thinking of the other side is pro-active. And for all I know, maybe, likewise, there are people at the boards who consider the union's side of the story before it is presented to them in the form of a protest, petition, or grievance. It should also be noted that studies now show that there is a correlation between mood and how much visual information we take in (this explains why lucky people find parking spots and money, I guess. Your affirmation here could be: "I open my eyes to all possibilities.").

3) Go ahead, slack off (this means not to try too hard and be too stubborn where you miss out on other paths to success, something we need to start teaching our students! Interestingly, Webber refers to an experiment where Wisemen (wrote *Luck Factor*) "conducted an experiment in which he gave subjects a newspaper and asked them to count how many photographs were inside. There were 43, and most subjects found them within a few minutes.

However, they could have completed the task within seconds had they read the large type on the second page of the paper. It said "stop counting- there are 43 photographs in this newspaper." Or they could have instead earned $250 had they noticed the half-page message that said "Stop counting, tell the experimenter you have seen this and win $250.'" Here is where it gets complicated because the moral of the story is that we know it is bad to procrastinate but if we sidetrack, sometimes we will catch lucky breaks. This is something that, in our culture, is harder with age because we feel trapped where we are. I had a co-worker tell me that teachers are trapped in their job because they will lose out on their pension if they leave. But this is a negative affirmation. It's like saying "I'm 40 years old, I'm too old to start playing a certain sport" or "I'm 33 and single, I'll never get married." Louise Hay is 84 years old and every several years she not only writes a new book which is what she has always been gifted at, but she takes up a new hobby such as changing her handwriting, taking ball room dancing and art lessons (etc). You can inspire yourself by always bettering yourself. Always have goals. And there is your affirmation, "I always have goals. I love my goals, I have no reason to regret and every reason to be gracious.").

4) Say Yes (if you're like me this makes you think of the film *Yes Man* and that movie is a comedy of course but it's not far off; be fearless about trying new things so as not to collect regret. Your affirmation here need be: "I am accomplishing my goals and in fact I am exceeding my own expectations. I am aware that good outcomes increase self-efficacy. I accomplish whatever I set out do, I accomplish whatever I set out to do.").

5) Embrace failure (Failure is a teacher. Your affirmation here needs to be: "All is well, the universe is unfolding as it should, all is well because I know that when an opportunity slips away that just means a new one comes along).

Remember, your cells are very aware of every thought you have. Our body is always talking to us. The dysfunctional disruptive student has stress in his/her life and that stress is transferable to you on many levels if you are not careful. It's harder still if you are not physically healthy to begin with, so you need to choose to think thoughts that create a healthy atmosphere both in you and around you. An example of a health affirmation is: "I love every cell of my body and I make healthy choices." For more listen to the Louise Hay CD "I Can Do It" or "Have Your Good Now" or read her book *Heal Your Body*.

When our stress is associated with hating someone or something it is literally dangerous. Holding on to pain is a powerful negative energy, one where we can feel the stress deteriorating our health and one where others can glance at us and know we don't feel good. Most teachers have experienced feelings of hate for a student, it's no fun admitting this, but we need to forgive any student who has deeply offended us and forgive ourselves and each other. And then this becomes easier. Live the best way you know how and affirm this. Release all perceived wrongs with love just as you would want your students to do. You have a choice. Will you willingly forgive the past?

Incidentally, on the bright side, we may see in our lifetime, a dramatic decrease in stress levels on our planet. In James O'Dea's essay, "You Were Born for Such a Time as This", he talks about a quickening in our collective consciousness in that there will be manifestations of peace and enlightenment after 2012. He states four points that are at the core of being mindful that more and more we are accessing because we are realizing that we are capable of these things. I think of my IDC4O class and that these points read like curriculum expectations:

-"Read the contents of our own hearts and minds" (student is self-aware)
-"Discern in each other's eyes an undiminished capacity for compassion" (if we can teach students this, not so many of them will give us teachers such a hard time all the time!)

-"Heed our persistent capacity for truth telling in the face of unprecedented manipulation."

-"Cultivate forgiveness for those who have harmed us or sought to suffocate our dreams" (this leads to prolonged alleviation of stress and is the most important point of the four; we need to teach students this life skill and we need to be very mindful of it ourselves within the confides of our union and workplace (I can think of one former principal who literally tried to suffocate my dreams by literally trying to push me out of the profession and there was a time where I had no interest in forgiveness. That is the past and like our thoughts, how we view the past can be changed so that it no longer has a negative imprint). It's taken me ten years in this profession to realize that the old quote is true that nobody can offend you without your permission, so I give my permission less often and this in turn creates a life with less stress. Furthermore, those around me may or may not notice that I am offended less often now, they will notice more if they are mindful but if they are not they will have old perceptions of me to go by and if I am mindful of this, I am understanding of this).

I said that blame is a negative affirmation. We should get out of the business of blaming students. *The Power* is wise to point out that: "If you get annoyed because there was a mix-up in an appointment, and you blame the other person for the mix-up, you are using blame as your excuse not to give love." This doesn't mean we have to ignore everything bad. I think there is such a thing as mindful complaining. I can complain on 9-11 by saying we need to do more to prevent terrorism. And when it comes to retail and services like the *Power* example, keep writing those complaint letters if it is necessary and/or if you are offering a constructive criticism, not blame (state so directly in your letter) based on actual experiences that will result in improved service that will benefit everyone not just you. *The Power* accurately tells us that: "Blame, criticism, finding fault, and complaining are all forms of negativity." However, as teachers we must critique work of students, we must find fault when a student has broken the rules, and we must complain about the things that need to change when our collective agreement expires. Again, here, we must be mindful that the intent behind these things is positive and altruistic. We mustn't have a chip on our shoulder against any student, parent, or the board. At least with retail and services we have the freedom to boycott if that is the only way to avoid complaining that store or company. When you catch yourself complaining about any of the following things, end with something positive, even if it's looking forward to improvement:

-weather

-your luck

-your height or weight

-the government

-the board

-the union

-other teachers

-students and/or their parents

-your partner

-your children

-your parents

-long lines (try reading a book while in line or go on the Internet on your cell phone, or write the store and say, "I would be more excited to shop at your store if you had more than just 2 people working the express lane since you have 6 cash stations there.")

-food (but use common sense; if you find a sharp object in your food, don't ignore that, it's serious and needs to be brought to the attention of management).

-your work

-customers

-businesses

-the local transit system

-prices

-noise

-service

Avoid taking offense from something someone says that you know they did not intend in an offensive way. Don't use words like terrible, horrible, disgusting, and awful unless you are sure that everyone would agree with you. You could use some of these words to describe gas prices but there are Europeans, pedestrians, and environmentalists who would disagree with you. You might call a student a menace but you would also know that not all his/her teachers will agree with that assessment and I'm sure neither would all his/her family and friends. The scary thing is "All that we send into the lives of others comes back into our own" so said poet Edwin Markham. This means two things: 1) when someone passes judgment on us we can brush it off with the knowledge that their karma is their business and 2) this means that if we try to get someone in trouble we are asking for trouble. Many of you have YouTubed "United Breaks Guitars." A man a couple years ago had his guitar loaded on a flight only to find it was broken afterwards. The airline refused to pay for the damage. They should have. It was bad business karma. The musician made a music video and catchy tune that gets stuck in my head every time I hear it:

United!!

You broke my Taylor guitar...

You broke it, you should fix it, You're liable just admit it

I should have flown with someone else OR GONE BY CAR....

'Cause United breaks guitars!

Within a day, millions of people had seen it and it even was featured on CNN! Unfortunately, the song made reference to an actual employee who received many threatening phone calls but the maker of the video posted a follow-up apology and implored people not to contact her. The singer in this case, I would suggest, did something in life to attract the breaking of the guitar, perhaps complained about something or didn't help someone when given the opportunity to but United attracted the flack into their life when they chose not to rightfully compensate the gentleman.

Stress Resources:

1. www.mybrainsolutions.com

2. Hayhouse.com (also see the bibliography of this book for suggested readings)

3. Teacher's Rule Facebook group

4. Abilify is FDA-approved to treat depression as add-on treatment

to an anti-depressant in adults when an antidepressant alone is not enough.

5. Employee Assistance Program goal orientated therapy.

6. Read *Your Birthday Your Card* (Administrators are obsessed with mitigating circumstances but we should as teachers not shy away from this ourselves. We should endeavor to find the mitigating circumstances in another's behaviour. It can be a tool in the battle against stress to. I love this book, it can help you understand yourself but I think more importantly it can help you understand your students, if you are like me and believe that there is some truth to numerology and astrology but even if you are not, science backs up the fact that certain conditions and personality traits are linked to birth months due to subtle influences on fetal brain development due to factors including sleep and wake cycles and the prevalence of viruses that differ from season to season (for example, summer babies grow up to be more open-minded and less neurotic. May is the luckiest month of all which makes perfect sense to me since one of the luckiest people I know is my oldest sister who was born in May).

7. http://www.oprah.com/spirit/How-Parents-Can-Help-Their-Children-Be-Stress-and-Anxiety-Free-Wayne-Dyer/7 (Oprah on anxiety and children)

8. "I love life." This is your default go to affirmation to use as an anti-venom to stress (how many times have you been stressed out and said or thought "FML" or "Life sucks" or maybe even, "I hate my life." ? I know I have been there done that. It takes seconds to counter this with: "I love life" or "I love this life."

9. http://www.theaffirmationspot.com/teachers.html (Teacher Affirmation site)

10. You have to read *Happy For No Reason* by Maria Shimoff who I talked about at the start of this chapter. It really truly is practical. She brilliantly teaches us to take responsibility for

our happiness. I learned in a clear perspective from her book and her talk that it is easy to overcome the myth of "I'll be happy when…" This is a wait for something outside of ourselves (i.e. that ten percent I quoted earlier). I used to think I will be happier when I am on vacation or when I lose weight or when I made more money. I admit it. But it is far more conducive to avoiding stress by shifting to seeing obstacles as lessons and therefore gifts!

11. Read *It's The Thought That Counts* by David R. Hamilton, PhD. He does a good job explaining how your body will produce less stress hormones by thinking positive thoughts. He also talks about the benefits of Reiki.

CHAPTER 22

JUDGMENT VS. DISCERNMENT

Most people know how to judge behavior and not the person themselves. We as humans discriminate more often then our conscious minds will allow us to admit. I implore schools and school boards to book Malcolm Gladwell as a guest speaker who can articulate this better than I can. But then there is the issue of discernment. My school board always was insisting that we teachers assess knowledge but also understanding and application. How can we expect students to discern instead of judge if we ourselves do not? In case you are thinking to yourself 'don't they both mean the same thing?" they are very different because of their outcomes. I once had to eject two students from my ENG3C class for their behavior during a final exam. A final exam for goodness sakes! It was the first time in nine years I had to eject a student in an exam let alone two students. The rest of the class was as quiet as a mouse which you would expect of any class in a final exam that is worth fifteen percent of the final grade to be, even ENG3C. And later that day, I recall saying to a couple of teachers, "if you can't even behave in a final exam, there is something very seriously wrong with your brain." Or something to that effect. The affirmation there is "misbehaving during a final exam is crazy, therefore the students who misbehave during a final exam are crazy. It's not true. On any given final exam in any given school, students are ejected for many many different reasons. I suspect that in most cases, the student knows that s/he has no way to excel on the exam. Discernment considers that last part because it operates under the "Law of Attraction."

I had a co-worker tell me once that "humans are amebas and one percent of us are giants." He went on to clarify that he considered himself among such intellectual giants. He must be the lowest paid "giant" on his list of that one percent he shares that stage with I thought. My negative affirmation was a reflex response to his negative and absurd if not delusional affirmation because I was re-affirming that there are "giants" but these so-called giants are not teachers. When we view ourselves as very smart, it is a powerful affirmation, but when we view ourselves as superior, it is often because during our upbringing we were praised and given the impression that we were generally smarter than most people in our lives. I do not speak from experience here, I always had friends, family, and co-workers who I thought were smarter than myself but regardless, we can ignore professional development opportunities if we deem them beneath us. Some teachers have no patience for first year teachers coming out of Teachers College because these veteran teachers have a pre-conceived notion that new teachers think that they have newer and superior knowledge that trumps experience. It is a gross generalization and stereotype. Affirm: "I seek out experts in areas that are outside of my expertise when needed." Also, since discrimination is self-serving and the opposite of this is serving others, affirm: "I am service- orientated."

While we are on the topic of judgment vs. discernment, please note that without recognizing it for what it is (negative affirmation) teachers often develop a strong "why bother" attitude towards things like discipline, failing a student, designing field trips, extra-curricular participation, filling out safe school forms or professional development feedback forms. They perceive a lack of support from the government and/or administration as justification. They are essentially judging and giving up on the system bettering itself. Yet, we know the system won't fix itself any more than the world will fix itself. To put this in perspective, consider the following text from Bruce Lipton in *Spontaneous Evolution- Our Positive Future*: "We all want to change the world, whether we realize it or not. On a conscious level, many of us feel inspired to save the planet for altruistic or ethical reasons. On an unconscious level, our efforts to serve as Earth stewards are driven by a deeper, more fundamental behavioral programming known as the *biological imperative-* the drive to survive... Consciously or unconsciously, most of us accept our own powerlessness and fragility in a seemingly out-of-control world. We perceive ourselves as mere mortals, just trying to make it through the day. People, on presuming helplessness, frequently beseech God to solve their problems. The image of a caring God deafened by a never ending cacophony of pleas emanating from this ailing planet was amusingly portrayed in the movie *Bruce Almighty,* in which Jim Carrey's character, Bruce, took over God's job. Paralyzed by prayers playing endlessly in his mind, Bruce transformed the prayers into Post-It notes only to become buried under a blizzard of sticky paper... our sense of disempowerment is the result of *learned limitations.*" If Lipton is right in his theory, and I believe he is, I am concerned that we as teachers may be enablers of this type of phenomenon. As teachers, we can run the risk of unwittingly disempowering our students by not encouraging them to utilize the power inherent in the mind.

Lipton isn't easy on us teachers just as teachers are not easy on parents in the blame game of why students make the choices they often do that is clearly not in their best interest. And in terms of health, Lipton states: "...Teachers and doctors programmed us with the belief that our cells and organs are frail and vulnerable. Bodies readily break down and are susceptible to sickness, disease, and genetic dysfunction. Consequently, we anxiously anticipate the probability of disease and vigilantly search our bodies for a lump here, a discoloration there, or any other abnormality that signals our impending doom." What we should be teaching our students is that our thoughts create our reality pure and simple. Thoughts affect us directly. Lipton goes on to talk about the phenomenon of fire- walking. Case after case, people who walk on coals get burned when they expect to get burned and experience no burns when they don't expect to get burned. I am convinced that if a student expects to fail a course they will get a final mark between a 0 and a 50. If a teacher expects a student to fail a course one thing is for sure, the student will either fail or barely pass. Surely, you can see the disconnect between discernment and judgment.

"Judge a man by his questions rather than his answers." Voltaire

CHAPTER 23

RELIGIOUS

...one person can walk into a room with love, and hundreds or maybe thousands absorb that love, and carry it out of the room with them. The love of the original bearer is not only undimished but has, very likely, increased. If ever there was a formula for applying the miracle of loaves and fishes, this is it!
-Spontaneous Evolution-

I should preface this chapter by saying that if you are anti-religion you may want to skip over this chapter however I encourage you to be open to it because religion can be a teacher on many levels. Also, during this chapter I will make reference to Adam and Eve and if you are like me, the Genesis story is one which you do not read literally but for argument's sake, we will pretend.

But first off, The Dali Lama says his religion isn't a religion at all, it is a practice. For this chapter, we will put semantics aside. When I went to the Louise Hay Hayhouse *I Can Do It Conference* in Toronto in May 2010, I was surprised that the first topic that the first speaker spoke on was of a religious nature. Dr. Dyer spoke about Padre Pio. He talked about the importance of us keeping in mind that all being comes from non-being and that each of us is a spark of God. What I am getting at, is I think religion is not as bad a word as detention and yet we often think the other way around in the world of education. Religion is not a bad word because as Dyer indicated, there are universal truths that Jesus, for example, spoke of.

After all these years in the business, I know that not much good comes out of detentions (at least not for the repeat-offenders). And after all these years of teaching world religions, I have a pretty good idea what all religions have in common. The HRT World Religions course in my Catholic school board does a wonderful job covering this but it is only one course, one semester out of at least eight semesters of high school. There are of course lots of things all religions have in common but they all teach love. I don't know what students are feeling and thinking about when they leave detention, I only ever had one in my life and that was when I was in grade eleven. I was late for Environmental Science class because I was talking to a girl in the hall who I had a huge crush on. I seem to recall thinking that the detention was worth it. If a detention is not viewed as a consequence by the student it will not be a deterrent. When students leave the World Religions class, at least some of them will reflect a great deal on the universal messages of love. I notice this even more so when I taught the class on line to summer school students. All of whom passed the course with flying colors.

The first thing I ever taught was grade seven Religion. And I remember having to teach the concept of "original sin." And some years later, again "original sin" was the basis of another course I taught, this time a grade twelve Religion course where the text book was so ultra-conservative and old-fashioned that I thought to myself the course should be called "How To Become a Catholic Priest." But it was satisfactory enough a text to teach the course. Nevertheless, original sin (which for those of you who are non-Christian, refers to, in a nut-shell, Adam and Eve in the Garden of Eden committing the first sin and thereby passing on to each human born since, the disease of sin) is a very important lesson to teach as it turns out after all. It is true that we all have pre-conceived attitudes about humanity and the universe that disable us from being positive 100% of the time. As an English teacher, I can tell you that the word 'sin' is defined as an "offense against God" but I can also tell you that it originally meant "missing the mark." Interesting, isn't it? As teachers, we use that term, "missing the mark."

Let's go back to the Adam and Eve story. They were punished in the Garden of Eden. But we can't possibly know how they were punished if we weren't there. We all know, I mean everyone with a grade eight-level education alive knows to some extent, that punishment can sometimes do more harm than good. There is clearly less of it in schools now then ever before and that is a good thing because we have gotten rid of zero-tolerance policies and corporal punishment and yelling. Punishment has been removed from schools for the wrong reasons in some cases in my opinion. Students who miss the mark don't need to be punished but they do not need to be rewarded either. Punishment is not found in nature and in society we have two extremes, we have the death penalty in many countries and some states (firing squad, electric chair gas chamber (etc)). Punishment in and of itself, does not work. If it did we would have eliminated all crime by now without question. It does not work because there is no change in consciousness and thinking patterns on the part of the accused. Notice that the Bible indicates that Adam and Eve were not consigned to Hell? But I wonder how many Christians mistakenly assume that they were-- all because they were defiant of God's law. Adam and Eve's first negative emotion was shame. Our pain bodies, our egos, our initial reactions to students often desire the student(s) to feel shame for their actions. There is no learning in a negative emotion like shame or guilt. Adam and Eve probably learned more in the garden than they get credit for.

In my experience, all schools seem to have detentions. I have had detention duty enough times to know that they do anything except work! Look at the detention-duty logs. It's the same names week after week after week from September to June. We need to replace this with teaching students about positive life skills and the knowledge of karma. We associate that word (karma) with a particular religion (especially Catholic school students in grade eleven and twelve who learn about world religions and learn about that term in the context of the Hindu faith). But it is a general term that refers to life being governed by the law of attraction, i.e. what you give, think, and say come back to you. If you never talk about anyone behind their back, nobody will ever talk about you behind your back in theory though being a public figure would be an exception to this example but I use this example because children and teens and young adults have no concept of karma on this level. When we look at how many grievances there are in any given year in any given board so to we can see that we need to be mindful of karma. I have never heard anyone argue or make a case against karma.

It simply is true that you get what you give. If you are mindful you will see that statement and convert it into an affirmation: "I get what I give and I give service to others." Sometimes, as even principals and superintendents will admit, there needs to be consequences. This is when students and their parents tend to get their back up the most. Yet, if we taught karma, then people will be more willing to accept consequences.

Adam and Eve must have accepted their consequences for humanity to continue. So it was because of learning that we are alive today. After reading Malcolm Gladwell's work, you can conclude that life in short, is about missing the mark and then taking better aim. This applies to academics and athletics as well in which case taking better aim involves visualization affirmations.

I for one was never an athlete. I was and am short with small arms and there are no athletes in my immediate family. I used to play soccer when I was a kid and I was pretty good. I won a couple of trophies. And when I was in grade five, I remember not paying attention anymore and I noticeably underperformed, needless to say I did not get very many goals that year, in fact if I recall, I didn't get any. And so, I quit. I missed the mark. I didn't bother to take aim. I used to be a horrendous bowler. Then I tried visualizing getting strikes each time I went to bowl a ball with my eyes closed and my scores continue to improve (the first time I tried it I did it in a child's lane with bumpers (i.e no gutter) which sounds funny but it's OK, I knew "in my mind" that I couldn't get strikes in the regular lane and so I had to start somewhere). Though I still can't for the life of me put a basketball in a net so I resign to that fact of reality but I do not deny that I could get better at basketball if I were to become dedicated to doing so. Missing the mark followed by improving oneself is what our focus should be. And that is what I think religion in general was about in the beginning and it is returning to that focus point.

Furthermore, the story of Adam and Eve is captivating on many levels. The temptation that Adam faced is almost unimaginable. I remember saying to a priest in Confession once, "Father, I know the Bible quotes Jesus as saying 'you will never be tempted beyond what you are capable of rejecting' but I don't understand how this can be true." I forget what his response was but whatever it was, it would not be until about a decade later when I started to realize the beauty and truth of Jesus' words that I just paraphrased.

Temptation and mind over matter could be a whole series of books just on that. When students misbehave, ultimately, they are "giving in", giving into temptation to misbehave. If a teacher is unorganized and has a cluttered classroom and seems tired and does not have a particular commanding presence, the temptation is much higher. Hopefully, by this point in the book, you have an idea that a classroom where affirmations are used by the teacher, provides an environment where the likelihood of this sort of temptation is far lessened. But it will never be 100% free of temptation. We should be realistic. I have an uncle who is a Catholic Monseigneur who has said, "Where there are humans, there is humanity." And whenever someone brings up mistakes or wrongdoings on the part of the Catholic Church he correctly says, "If you were 2000 years old you would have made mistakes along the way too."

In the public schools, Jesus is usually not spoken of and in the Catholic schools, the majority of students by the time they are in high school feel as though religion is being forced on them and they do not want to take Religion courses. When the Chaplin came into my ENG3C class to do a preamble with them the day before our homeroom Mass, he asked them, "Why do we go to Church?" And several students responded: "Because we have to."

But what Jesus said about love, forgiveness, and faith we need to start brushing up on. My favorite Bible verse for as long as I can remember has always been when Jesus said of faith, "If you had faith the size of a mustard seed you could commend the mountains to move and they would obey you." I remember in one of my religion courses I took at the University of Ottawa, the Prof (who was/is also a Catholic deacon) was reading this passage and building it up in his lesson in an inspiring way and then asked the class, "So does this mean we can move mountains?" And you had a sense that everyone in the room was on the verge of yelling back: "YES!" But he got blank stares instead and he said, "Of course not!" It is symbolic. But make no mistake about it, Jesus often reiterated through his parables that we need to overcome our limiting beliefs. We can do this through a deep understanding of love, forgiveness, and faith, and understanding that must always be open to expanding.

When I saw Billy Graham live in person in Ottawa in 1998, there was one night during his crusade where he said, "Tonight, I want to talk about a battle that is going on in your mind. There are two great forces." He went on to talk about how there is a battle of good versus evil and only one can lead to inner peace. Billy has spent his whole life studying the Bible and has concluded what proponents of affirmations and mindfulness are saying.

Other relevant Billy Graham quotes that he made in Ottawa and at other crusades in the past:

-"The end of the world could be a thousand years away or it could be tomorrow. The end of the world will come to you when YOU die. What have you done to prepare for that moment when your heart stops beating and your brain waves stop?"

-"Try to forgive. I never hold a grudge. In fact, many people say that I never get angry."

-"My calling is to preach the love of God and the forgiveness of God and the fact that he does forgive us."

-"I think it is a sin to look at another person as inferior to yourself because of race or because of ethnic background."

-"It is not the body's posture, but the heart's attitude that counts when we pray."

-"Our days are numbered. One of the primary goals in our lives should be to prepare for our last day. The legacy we leave is not just in our possessions, but in the quality of our lives. What preparations should we be making now? The greatest waste in all of our earth, which cannot be recycled or reclaimed, is our waste of the time that God has given us each day."

-"Courage is going from failure to failure without losing enthusiasm."

-"A child who is allowed to be disrespectful to his parents will not have true respect for anyone."

-"A real Christian is a person who can give his pet parrot to the town gossip."

-"Believers, look up - take courage. The angels are nearer than you think."

-"Give me five minutes with a person's checkbook, and I will tell you where their heart is."

-"God will prepare everything for our perfect happiness in heaven, and if it takes my dog being there, I believe he'll be there."

-"Man has two great spiritual needs. One is for forgiveness. The other is for goodness."

-"Nothing can bring a real sense of security into the home except true love."

-"Tears shed for self are tears of weakness, but tears shed for others are a sign of strength."

-"When wealth is lost, nothing is lost; when health is lost, something is lost; when character is lost, all is lost."

I know both the Billy Graham Evangelical Association and the Catholic Church have been talking more and more about eco-theology and what religion in general has to say about nature and the environment. Interestingly, the more mindful one is, the more concerned they are for our planet. Why is this so? And isn't this a very ancient inner calling? As stated in *Spontaneous Evolution- Our Positive Future*, "Animism is, perhaps, the closest that humankind has come to balancing its emphasis on spirit and matter since the Garden of Eden." The world's first religion essentially taught that we are children of the earth (Jesus said, "You are the salt of the earth, the light of the world."), that our purpose here is to thrive, and that we must live in balance with nature.

If students in both Catholic and public schools continue to view religion as useless, out of date, judgmental, and based on myth rather than truth then it will be increasingly difficult for them to be open to something like affirmations. Not that all people who are indifferent or anti-religious are closed-minded. But it can be a natural progression.

My Catholic parents believe in the Rapture, though it is not a Catholic belief, and I think we need to ask ourselves why more and more people (depending on which statistics you view, up to 80% of Americans) believe in this prophesied phenomenon. Moreover, why so many students speak of 2012 (even before the blockbuster movie came out, actually it was the *X-Files* that first introduced the concept to popular culture back in 2002, when the Smoking Man said to Scully, "the truth Mulder has sought scared the Myans so much that my story begins where their calendar ends, Dec.21st, 2012."). When the 2010 magnitude 5 earthquake struck the Ottawa area, I witnessed many students saying that it was the beginning of 2012 (some were more serious than others of course). In the documentary, *Jesus Camp*, it is amazing to see the state of and resurgence of religious fundamentalism. People have become obsessed with the end-times, the Rapture, and apocalyptic thinking. Of course this isn't always a good thing and it makes sense why "religion" is a considered a "bad word" by some like Bill Maher who warned about what he called "self fulfilling prophecies" in his documentary, *Religilous*.

Though as anti-religious as Bill Maher is, he is open-minded enough to admit that Jesus' most famous quote known as the Golden Rule is an important universal truth ("Do unto others as you would have them do unto you"), whereas there are some students we teach that clearly and directly do not agree with the philosophy. There is a simple test you can do with students, ask them what they would do if they won $50 million in a lottery. Then ask them "How much would you give to charity?" And you may be surprised at how many of them say, "I would give back to charity as much as charity has given me, $0."

So many people are priding themselves and considering themselves enlightened by dismissing religion and yet religion is becoming more and more focused on social justice and peace whereas in the secular world, our politicians have other priorities which is not seemingly a problem based on voter turn-out. At the 2010 G20 Conference in Toronto (where well over $1 billion was spent on security and where 900 protesters were arrested!), very little that was on the agenda was covered, the politicians spent most of their time discussing the idea of an international bank tax. So water crisis, poverty, environment, and corporate crime just are not that important. How the US President can sleep at night while a company like Monsanto is permitted to do what they do is unsettling, well no, it's down right sickening. If you don't know what Monsanto does Facebook or Google it.

Religion in general goes to show that universal love is unconditional. We are loved no matter what. That is an affirmation: "We are loved no matter what." So we do not need to climb up 100 steps on our knees with a rosary in our hand at the Oratory of St. Joseph in Montreal though this can be a wonderful meditative prayer for some people who are physically capable of doing that particular pilgrimage, and we certainly do not need to fast or whip ourselves though again, different meditations work for different people. One of the greatest Popes of all time, the late Pope John Paul II practiced self-flagellation. That is something I have a hard time understanding and I would never ever consider doing it myself probably or mainly because that might draw blood and just typing the word blood right now gives me a headache because I have a blood-phobia that some of you can no doubt relate to but I'm willing to bet that my phobia is attributed to a past life experience I had that involved me being seriously harmed or killed in a bloody or gory manner and a past life regression could cure this but that's neither here nor there and you do not have to believe in re-incarnation.

Jesus also said, "The meek shall inherit the earth." In our schools, students are so competitive. Competition can be healthy but when it is not it gets in the way of mindfulness. Watch students play video games for example and observe. And look at the types of video games that they are playing too while you're at it. There's nothing mindful about playing a game where the object of said game involves shooting people in an airport. But we don't seem to be addressing this in schools. I once had a behavior problem student use an app on his phone to take a picture of me in class without permission that automatically edited the picture to make it appear that I had been shot in the head! Disrespect is the opposite of mindfulness.

Jesus said "Blessed are the peacemakers." This is one of the beatitudes. I think we are called to be people of the beatitudes and I think holism expands on these teachings. Holism is all about taking care of each other and the planet. We need to be focused on promoting peace if we are to take care of each other and the planet. We have a long way to go assuming we have come a long way. If we haven't, we have even further to go. Billy Graham has said we are no closer to world peace then we were when we were mostly savage tribes. I remember seeing a video posted on YouTube and Facebook shortly after the 2010 G20 in Toronto where hundreds of citizens were standing or sitting in the street singing their national anthem, "Oh Canada" (which includes the lyrics: "God keep our land glorious and FREE...") and there was about twenty feet of space and then an equal amount of riot police on foot, bike, and horse just standing there still during the entire rendition. Immediately, at the end of the song, the police began firing rubber bullets and charging into the peaceful crowd like bullies, pushing, hitting, and arresting. Why I had to see this on YouTube and Facebook and why it was never broadcasted on TV is not shocking to me of course, I do teach media literacy after-all, but talk about unsettling! We are not free at all. Mediocrity is a growing problem. What we are now left with is a society governed by silly and cruel policies in which our politicians are affirming anything but peace. They are affirming fear, control, and tyranny insuring that there will always be poverty and war and ensuring that there will be a glaring omission of care when something like the BP Gulf of Mexico oil spill happens.

I remember learning a lot of good strategies to deal with conflict at D'Youville College in Buffalo, New York, when I was in Teachers' College. I remember learning that the most dysfunctional way to handle conflict is to be aggressive. I think the second most dysfunctional way is to be totally permissive and what I call a teacher pacifist. All this does is give your principal the false assumption that things are peachy-keen in your classroom but then s/he gets a call or letter from an irate parent who is as irresponsible or more so then their son or daughter and can only find blame with you the teacher for the 52% final mark on the report card. In this case, enforced detentions would have been better than no detentions at all. When a student skips a detention it is a perfect opportunity for a teacher to call a parent and work together in a positive way with the parent. Even cold and unreasonable parents are much more receptive early on as opposed to waiting until half way or later through a course. You can go a whole year without hearing a complaint from a parent by using affirmations. But sooner or later there will be one and it's important to keep the following in mind: we should feel sorry for the parents that blame teachers over and over again for their child's misbehavior and/or failure. We should not get our back up or take offense because in doing so we are doing what they are doing, that is, we are making ourselves victims. Parents who deny responsibility for how their son or daughter performs at school make themselves out to be victims and therefore they make affirmations of helplessness without even knowing it. Parents can't be any further from mindfulness when they blame teachers. Mindfulness, true mindfulness, you see, disengages automatic subconscious programs and then and only then, can we generate behavior that is coherent with our intentions. Furthermore, if you have an unreasonable parent to deal with each semester like clockwork, then you are not being mindful. I know it sounds pretentious of me to say that to you but trust me, this used to be me. I can look back at all the irate parents I have had to deal with most of whom I can remember, some I forget, and I also have kept old behavior logs which serve as a good reminder that most if not all of these would have been prevented if I was practicing mindfulness. You might know a teacher who is not familiar with mindfulness and who does not have behavior problems with students or parents. Well, scrap the word "might" we all do. This point is irrelevant as it does not debunk the value of mindfulness. It simply means that the teacher in question is an exemplary teacher or that they have a natural assertive presence that some or all around them find intimidating. Such teachers can't relate to the average teacher who does not fall into either of those two categories and so if they are quick to judge teachers who do experience behavior problems this goes to show that they are from being mindful. That is a negative affirmation that is and will continue to manifest problems either in the classroom or at home or in their physical health. Passing judgment is an old detrimental affirmation. The little judgmental mindsets aren't as little as you would think, they are like little white lies that bind together and add up over time. A classic example being when a teacher implies or outright tells me my class average is too high, it's all so silly.

Education has always been about knowledge. To have an effective knowledge base you need to have either book-smarts or street- smarts (life & learning skills). This is no longer good enough for the 21st century: "At present, humanity has vast amounts of knowledge, but still very little wisdom. Without developing wisdom, it is most unlikely that we will avoid catastrophe." Those words are taken from Peter Russell and his essay "A Singularity in Time" which I came across in a book called *2012*. Don't be fooled by the title. Nowhere in the book does it say the world will end on Dec.21st, 2012! The book has more to do with our potential in post-2012. Speaking of this wisdom, again here we can see that a course like the HRT World Religions usually comes across to the class that throughout human history there have been wise people, great people, people that were purely positive, the saints of course, mystics, lamas, prolific historical figures like

Ghandi, the list goes on. It is knowledgeable to know about them it is wise to learn from them because they knew better than us what the nature of consciousness was and is. Speaking of Ghandi, by the way, I always like to stress to the HRT class that it was Ghandi who said, "We need to be the change we want to see in the world." That is good advice in that one person can make a difference but it is also a grave warning. As I said in the affirmations chapter, one negative thought affects us but also goes out into the world and is added to our collective energy because it is energy and energy can't be destroyed in part because it is all interconnected but it can be converted. Our world can be converted. We can become the people of the Beatitudes.

It is wisdom when we stop repeating the same negative affirmation over and over again expecting different results and chose a new path or reboot and start from the beginning with positive affirmations. Let me use my laundry analogy. Once when my iron was broken, I did a load of laundry and there were several shirts and especially all my shorts that were extremely wrinkled. I tried putting them through the dryer to no avail and I tried hanging them in the bathroom while I ran the hot water for several minutes to the point of extreme steam to no avail. Finally, I put them back in the washer even though they were not dirty and started at square one and I got all the wrinkles out just as I had anticipated. Sometimes we need to go back to the beginning and start over. Russell goes on to put it best by stating: "... our minds are so full of scheming, planning, and worrying whether or not we will get what we think will make us happy, we seldom experience the peace and ease that lie at our core. When we awaken to our true nature, we are freed from dependence on the external world both for our sense of self and our inner being. We become free to act with more intelligence and compassion, attending to the needs of the situation at hand rather than the needs of the ego. We can access the wisdom that lies deep within us all." There is the affirmation: "I amass knowledge but I develop wisdom." And, "I access the wisdom that lies deep within me."

Daniel Pinchbeck wrote an essay called: "How the Snake Sheds Its Skin: A Tantric Path to Global Transformation" in which it is illustrated quite well that "we are being called upon to open our hearts, as well as our minds, to the radiant flame of transformation." How well equipped are we as teachers to sooth the world then? The teachings of Abraham-Hicks argues that soothing cannot take place outside the "vortex." The vortex is exactly where we need to be when we are in the classroom. Pinchbeck says, "Our ability to help the world and heal humanity's traumas depend upon the inner work we have done to master ourselves and attain equanimity of mind, or what Buddhism defines as nonattachment." Perhaps if I was more mindful when my car broke down I could have had a more Buddhist approach and saw the humor in it. "Buddha taught that suffering arises out of feeling separate. To the degree that we identify as a separate self, we have the feeling that something is wrong, something is missing. We want life to be different from the way it is. An acute sense of separation—living inside of a contracted and isolated self—amplifies feelings of vulnerability and fear, grasping and aversion. Feeling separate is an existential trance in which we have forgotten the wholeness of our being" (See: http://www.tarabrach.com/articles/inquiring-trance.html)

People often say prayer doesn't work. If they say that it's like saying affirmations don't work in which case they won't work. Mindfulness in prayer can prove this wrong. Here's how I sometimes pray:

Dear God: I love you, my family, friends, co-workers, and all people I encounter. Thank you for everything that has ever been created. I have every reason to be thankful at all times and no reason to be offended or resent you or myself. FORGIVE ME for when I have been the one to cause offense or whenever I have given in to a bad temper. I certainly wish to indicate to you my sincere desire to undue any bad karma as a result of BLASPHEMEY on my part, Lord.

I am proud to be your Son and I know in my heart that you understand my impatience considering my genetic programming and my list of extenuating circumstances that have been present in my life (list your specific examples here). Creator and Divine: Jesus I trust in You; Jesus I trust in You; Jesus I trust in You. Lord, honestly, Forgive me of my blasphemy and inconsiderate behavior and choices. Do help me remove it from my programming.

I pray Lord for my current prime directive that I am always happy with my wife as I am now. I pray that I accomplish my prime directive by always being mindful with your support. I also take this time to invite you to stand by me as I lose weight and enhance my health. For love and joy and lots of it in my life I pray, For me, my friends, family, co-workers, students and all people, for inner peace in their lives. I seek You. I seek peace and love with you. Please listen to me, please hear me, please consider what I have gone through. HELP ME BE MINDFUL.

That I successfully ____________________ (list specific/current tasks). God, I thank you for the opportunity to call upon the support of MARY... Mary, help me master the elimination of stress in my job and life; may the Lord grant me the happiness and joy that life has to offer. Mary, pray for all of us. I pray for all those in need. I pray for my friends and family in a particular way for their health and happiness. For my rapport with my students, co-workers, friends, and family. l try to be a good person and have faith in you and faith that I have chose a profession that can help make the world a better place. I want to live a long happy life. For those closest to me __________________ (discuss the needs of those closest to you). I thank you for this gift of suffering that although I do not understand I have faith that it has made me a better person. I am through suffering now Lord so help me to be happy now. I pray that the world makes a quantum leap forward in how it views people. Let all discrimination end. I pray for energy Lord. As a teacher, I always need it. Please let me tap into energy. Make me a better teacher. by enhancing my organizational skills and energy levels.

I pray that you will help me be organized in my teaching career. Blessings upon my family and friends and students and co-workers es. my parents, my sisters, and friends and those I know who especially need to be prayerfully considered: __________________ (list those you know who are in poor physical or mental health). Bless my car. Bless my classroom. For the teachers of Canada. For those who have died especially the dearly faithfully departed souls of ______________________ (list names here). For my current and past students... For my future students...

That I overcome any and all addictions, also for good health. May I meet the needs of my students

Thank you for answered prayers (including ____________________________ (list them here)).. Thank you Lord for the gift of humor. That the human race will make a quantum leap forward away from genetically programmed and culturally conditioned prejudices. Thank you for patience and the opportunities to become patient.

For an increase in faith, health, love, hope and charity. May I always be thankful for the family, friends, co-workers, and students I have had. Thanks for those students who have made me smile so much.

Help me in a divine way with my goals and affirmations, es.: ___________ (list actual affirmations here). Let it be known that I am truly grateful with great graciousness for answered prayers and realized affirmations including: ___________________ (list them here). Dear God, Holy Spirit, Archangel Michael, all of my guides, and all of my angels, I ask that you speak to me. Watch over me. Please help me be a clear channel of Divine communication. Please help me to clearly hear, see, know, and feel accurate and detailed messages that will bring blessings to my partner and myself. Please boost my ability to clearly hear, see, think, and feel Your Divine communication. Please help me to accurately receive these messages, and to bring forth those that will bring blessings to me. I have faith that prayerful affirmations are true affirmations and work (without faith that they work, they do not work, because they can't). Lastly, assist me Oh Lord in being ever so cognizant of St. Augustine's words: "Faith is to believe that which you do not yet see; and the reward of this faith is to see that which you believe."

I pray that all my prayers and affirmations may be heard, considered, and answered in the name of Your Son, my Lord and Saviour, Jesus Christ, who lives and reigns with You and the Holy Spirit, one God forever and ever, Amen. (I usually begin and/or end with the Lord's Prayer (The Our Father)).

I think the Ontario Catholic School Graduate Expectations that are in place in Ontario's Catholic schools as designed in 1998 by the Institute for Catholic Education should be very proud of the efforts to produce graduates who are caring and who are reflective, creative and holistic thinkers which they define as someone who among other things, "creates, adapts; evaluates new ideas in light of the common good, thinks reflectively and creatively to evaluate situations and solve problems; makes decisions in light of gospel values with an informed moral conscience; adopts a holistic approach to life by integrating learning from various subject areas and expertise; and examines, evaluates and applies knowledge of interdependent systems (physical, political, ethical, socio-economic and ecological) for the development of a just and compassionate society." Some of the biblical inspiration behind this comes from 1 Peter 3, 15: "In an age, which seems more fearful of the future, we are dedicated to give an account of the hope that is within us."

You know, at the start of this book I talked about money and how it is neither the root of all evil nor is it the pathway to happiness. I recall Dr. Dyer quoting Shakespeare at the Toronto conference I was at, "A crown that seldom kings enjoy." As an English teacher I loved the reference and thought it wise that it be brought up since in this case, "crown" is a metaphor for contentment. Then Dyer said, "Your concept of yourself is the only way to elevate your life to a higher place." The next speaker at the conference, Gregg Bryden, talked about 2012 and the Myans and he also said, "The earth's magnetic field changed fifteen minutes after the first plane hit on 9/11." Our world is made of electromagnetic fields. This knowledge is bridging a gap between religion and science. The next speaker, Brian Weiss said, "We never really die, because we were never really born." The next speaker, Bruce Lipton talked about the history of religion and a progressive return to holistic thinking/holism and how America was once a deist nation. In a short period of time we have gone from reformation to science to deist to Darwinism to the DNA and human genome generation to where we are today. During that time our society has become pre-occupied with money and we need to be mindful that as Lipton pointed out, the Declaration of Independence couldn't work after 1860 when Americans went to a gold standard and the Civil War took place. And in terms of the human genome project, notice how religion cautioned us? Lipton said, "We were fooled by the venture capitalist pharmaceuticals (each gene is a drug)." Lipton pointed something out that has not worked its way in to most physical health curriculums, that being that while the #3 killer today is cancer and indeed the #2 killer is cardio-vascular disease, the #1 cause of death is iatrogenic (medicine). We know that the health industry saves lives but it also takes lives. Mindfulness will one day dramatically change these statistics in our lifetime. The next speaker was Carolyne Myss who has a Catholic background and talked about prayer. She said that when people say "why did this happen to me?" it is a negative affirmation because it puts yourself as the center of the universe and you don't care about anyone else when you think that way. It is here where you want justice to be yours. All religion teaches that you should not put God to the test and that you need faith. Myss said, "Healing comes from giving up the battle with God." She spoke of St. Theresa of Avala. She showed that you can't heal if you harm others. As Gord Downie said in the song *Love is a First,* "You get what you give, not deserve." Myss said, "Pride is the opposing force. We have the capacity to love all humanity but we need to compete or at least think we do." She spoke of the grace of knowing that "you have what it takes to recognize the God-spark in others (we all do, but sometimes we can't bear to see the other's God-spark). See them spark more often. Give them all you got, otherwise, it's greed..." Let us see the sparks in our students and colleagues! We unfortunately, tend to spend more time complaining about our students' generation's sense of entitlement but what are we doing to teach our students that this sense of entitlement leads to break-down? History has shown us this. The next speaker was Maria Shimoff who talked about what she calls "happiness for no reason" and which she acknowledged that Christianity calls this "the Kingdom of God within."

In closing of this chapter, go easy on religion, if it weren't for love, there would be no religion to begin with, so religion came of love and has given us such motivational people as St. Bernard of Clairvaux who said "The measure of love is love without measure." Having taught religion many times I know how irritated non-religious students get when it comes to religion. But getting irritated is a negative affirmation and we will need to do a better job teaching students this and we can't do that unless we ourselves complain less in life. Irritation is a barrier to success and a barrier to a healthy self-image. Joyce Chapman wrote in *The Live Your Dream Workbook*, "If you're not busy living to your fullest potential, parts of you are busy fading away." So many things can get in the way of meeting potential. And so many things can help us overcome or become immune to these things. Psychologist Dr. Garland Landrith, whose research was cited in the movie *What the Bleep Do We Know*, has discussed how inner thoughts can alter the physical realm through various methods including mass consciousness experiments, prayer, and "tapping" techniques. I'm not too familiar yet with tapping techniques, although my reiki- master sister once tried it on me to get rid of heartburn and I did not find it as effective as Nexium not that I even want to know what the side-effects are of Nexium. The side-effects of anything in life can depend on genetic factors and what we are thinking and feeling at the time in question. If we anticipate side-effects from something, we greatly increase the chance that there will be side-effects. Various studies have demonstrated the quantum effects of consciousness, indicating that the mind can go beyond the time/space limitations that the normal universe operates under. For instance, Dr. Garland Landrith has reported on an experiment in which people were randomly shown pleasant and negative photos. It was found that the subjects experienced anxiety several seconds in advance of seeing a negative photograph, which suggests the body senses things ahead of time, he said. Landrith has shown that people are often held back by psychological blocks-- brain patterns that cause them to make the same mistakes over and over again. This can explain a lot in terms of dumb things we have done in our lives and it can explain a lot about why students do things that they know perfectly well will lead to them getting in trouble. Through an Emotional Freedom Technique (EFT) that involves a person using their fingers to tap on various acupuncture points, these blocks can be removed, according to Landrith. This is something we may see implemented in schools in the future pending the support of further scientific studies. Further, I heard Landrith on *Coast to Coast* AM once where he cited the recent Dallas Peace Project, in which 1,000 people tapped on acupuncture points, and crime rates reportedly went down twenty-five percent in the region. Landrith also spoke about various prayer studies and techniques. Some particularly powerful methods include "releasing" an intention rather than focusing on it, posing an intention before going to sleep, and sending out feelings of love. By adopting a sense of gratitude-- being thankful for what you have, you'll be attracting more things to be grateful for than if you are in a state of wanting, which attracts lack, according to Landrith. As I implied earlier, it was Jesus who taught us that we have to model behavior. As teachers, we do this whether we want to or not, whether we realize it or not. We have to model moral behavior. "Young people are forming their self-image every day—based largely on the examples of self-respect and self-esteem they see in the important people in their lives." Wayne Dyer

CHAPTER 24

IDC4O MINDFUL HEALTHY LIVING

In the fall of 2010, I had the blessed experience of teaching a class that had never previously been taught. A course I designed. IDC4O: Interdisciplinary Studies: Mindful Healthy Living.

On the first day of class I had the students write a journal response to the following quote: "We attract not what we wish for, we attract who we are."

To illustrate that we don't always think things through mindfully, I had the students write down any three wishes they could have if they came across a genie in a lamp. You can imagine some of the things they wrote. This activity was inspired by an *X-Files* episode where someone wishes to be invisible and then meets an untimely end by being hit by a transport truck who couldn't see them, another wishes for a boat and the boat inconveniently appears on the front lawn, and Mulder wishes for world peace and is the only living thing left on the planet. In the end, Mulder figures it out; the only wish that would not have negative consequences would be to wish for the genie in the lamp to be freed. The altruistic wish can have no negative consequences.

Another activity I did was inspired by *The Shadow Effect* series. I had the students write down their best quality (for me I put "sense of humor") and then had them write down the opposite of that (for me that meant: "dry personality")... Most of the time, this ends up being a trait that the person hates. Also, we can see that it ends up being a trait we judge in others and you attract people like that. Then the students are asked to think about a person who annoys them the most. For me, I thought of a co-worker who came to mind at the time. Then the students determine what specific attribute it is that causes them to annoy (for me, the attribute was "arrogance"), next, the students point at the person, in their mind, and call them that attribute. They are then asked to notice that they have three fingers pointing back at them. The point being that you don't want to own or acknowledge that characteristic in yourself. Try the exercise yourself right now before you read on. Now ask yourself, what do you do to prove you are not that trait you despise in someone else? I know that I have often been way too non-assertive to the point that I get stressed-out or hate myself for not being assertive.

I had the students make a beautiful affirmations word-wall. One of the students wrote "I have the means to travel anywhere." I had a co-worker come into my classroom one day after school and noticed that particular affirmation and said, "What is this? Does this person have a private jet at their disposal!?" I laughed.

I showed the film *The Story of Ron Clark*. Ron Clark is an American teacher who has worked with disadvantaged students in rural North Carolina and Harlem, New York. He is known for his books on teaching children in middle schools. The students saw how Clark succeeded where so many teachers had failed because he had a positive mind-set and stubbornly stuck with it. In one scene in particular, Ron Clark says to his principal, "The problem isn't the kids, it's your expectations of the kids."

I showed the film *The Next Karate Kid* which is the fourth movie in that franchise. I can't think of a more conducive film. The main character is brought to a Buddhist monastery and taught the ways of mindfulness. Her days of being suspended from school thereafter were over.

I had the students participate in a group discussion on-line via the class website in several conversations but there was on in particular I posted after my car broke down, on all my class web site discussion boards that read: "Dear student of Mr. D'Alessio: Well as some of you may have heard, my car broke down Wednesday night when I was driving it. I had it temporarily fixed the next day but then later that night, it broke down again and died. On top of that, I lost my cell phone for the 100th time (maybe it was just the 77th time...). Based on what we have learned in the class (IDC4O: affirmations; ENG4C: great authors have used their bad experiences as their muse/inspiration/motivation to their writing; CH2P/L: in a historical context, people have found ways to be very happy and successful and prosper in times of war, depression, and set-backs... and based on your own experience, what do you think I should make of this. Here are some options I can think of:

a) I have always used prayer and affirmations to remind myself that bad luck happens to everyone and can't be avoided but in the end the universe will unfold as it should and there will be more good times then bad

b) not complain about my luck at all because there are billions of less fortunate people in the world that would be offended if they knew I was adopting a "woe is me" attitude (eg. 70% of people on the planet go to bed hungry each night, while other are mourning the loss of a loved one (etc).

c) Abandon the idea that prayers and affirmations can reduce events that cause stress.

d) Think to myself that thinking that I get more bad luck than the average person is just an illusion

e) Increase the amount of prayer and affirmations I use in my life

f) buy a lottery ticket

g) other"

I also posted the following: "Student & Teacher affirmation: I know that I am not perfect and therefore not every day is perfect but I am happy and successful and as such love getting up in the morning knowing the power a day can make moreover knowing that indeed each day is a new day. I know that I have important work to do and I choose to look forward to it. My work is challenging at times and that is a good thing. My work is deeply rewarding. I begin each day with a prayer and/or affirmation thereby blessing my situation with love. I am on a journey and there are stepping stones along the path. Some of those stones are negative experiences because of my thinking patterns being imperfect in accordance to my human nature. But in the end, I have more joy than sorrow. I take pride in my ability to connect with my Higher Power to make changes that bring more positive experiences into my life. I affirm my effort, energy, and organizational skills at school. I am thus always smiling, calm, productive, and allowing my cells to do their job easily by focusing on positive things rather than negative. My Higher Power works through me as I work at school."

I took the students to the Chapel once a month for meditation. Here is one example:

Lesson:

-Discuss: what is meditation?

-Discuss: Who meditates?

-Discuss different types of meditations. (Stress, religion, addiction, weight loss, money problems, health, past life regression, organization, communication, death, dreams, energy, feeling lost, forgiveness, love, peace, work, etc).

-Discuss steps in making a meditation (begin with a quote or reading (music or sounds is optional), quiet yourself, position yourself, relax body from head to toe, establish visual, narrative with your own wording, wording from pre-existing meditation(s), silence for reflection or prayer or just plain stillness, close with a quote, prayer, or ad lib narrative, etc).

-Meditation 2 IDC4O: Marianne Williamson said: "What we give to others, we give to ourselves. What we withhold from others, we withhold from ourselves. In any moment, when we choose fear instead of love; we deny ourselves the experience of Paradise." Please close your eyes and lie down or sit in a meditation position. You are on a space ship. You are the Captain of this space ship. You have a crew of explorers, scientists, and engineers. Your ship has twenty decks or floors. On the first deck, you have several holodecks

(A holodeck is a simulated reality. The students would have already learned this is grade eleven English with me when I taught them *Fahrenheit 451* by Ray Bradbury at which point I showed them the short film *The Veldt*. This short filmed took place in a holodeck. It was based on a Bradbury short story that was perhaps the first science fiction author to envision a simulated environment similar to the *Star Trek* holodeck that the term holodeck comes from. Bradbury wrote about a children's nursery that could create material objects based on thought.). On your time off, you can go into any of these holodecks. You are walking along the hall on the first deck and you enter the holodeck. You are in a 17th century Irish village, you walk through the town- square and come across a beautiful mansion, actually, it's a castle, you go inside, walk through the living room...... kitchen....solarium....you go outside into the garden following a stone path, it begins to rain but the rain does not bother you, it feels good, you see a fountain in the middle of the garden, you keep going, you see there is a pool, a hot tub, a sauna, and then there is an arch that seems out of place, it is a gateway to the rest of the holographic rooms.... You enter..... you are passing by some of these. On one there is an arcade, another is a wedding reception, the next has a carnival, the next a resort on a busy beach, followed by a quiet isolated cottage on a lake. Further down, there is a submarine under the water, another holodeck room appears to be an 18th century ship sailing along the ocean, the last room you come to is a cruise ship in Alaska, it's cold but beautiful. You stop and think about which of these you want to hang out in today, or maybe you want to go back to the garden or the Irish village or your room on the ship. Which will be the most fun or relaxing today? You pick one place and go there. After several minutes of peace and tranquility, you see three elderly people you do not recognize. You find this odd. You approach them and ask. "What are you doing here?" They reply: "waiting." You ask, "Waiting for what?" One of them responds: "You have too many questions." You walk past them. But then it dawns on you, they must be there for a reason. They must have something to teach me. You return. You ask them, "Is there something I can learn from you? And one of them says: "Everything you need comes to you in perfect time space sequence. Just as all the stars and planets are in their perfect orbit and in Divine right order, so are you. You may not understand everything that is going on with your limited human mind; however, you know that on the cosmic level, you must be in the right place at the right time, doing the right thing. Positive thoughts dominate here and so to must in your life, therefore they are what you choose to think. This present experience is a stepping stone to a new awareness and greater glory."

-Moment of silence and reflection

-Closing: Louise Hay affirmations meditation (p.9 from *Meditations to Heal Your Life*).

We have to teach students to learn to not listen to anyone who tells them they can't reach a goal. Our students are much more than we realize and they are much more than they realize! We forget this just as we forget that our universe is indescribable in its limitlessness. In season rhree of *The X-Files,* there is an episode ("Jose Chung is From Outer Space") where there are "Men in Black" one of whom is played by Jesse Ventura and at one point he says: "Your scientists have yet to discover how neural networks create self-consciousness, let alone how the human brain processes two-dimensional retinal images into the three-dimensional phenomenon known as perception. Yet you somehow brazenly declare that seeing is believing!" There will always be worlds and possibilities we cannot see. But we can imagine them. It is my hope that students learn that they can be whatever they want to be. Like so many of my students, I have gone through times were I saw myself as a victim, as someone less smart than my co-workers, as someone less attractive than my friends, not as talented as others, and I am thankful that I no longer paint that picture. If I still painted that picture I would not be writing this book.

I also did a simple journal activity whereby the students had to fill in the blanks (give it a try):

<u>I LOVE:</u>

Places:

Cities:

Countries:

People:

Colors:

Companies:

Services:

Sports:

Athletes:

Music:

Animals:

Flowers:

Clothes:

Food:

To do:

I also do an activity where they list ten things they feel they are entitled to. Air, legal representation, TV, water, rights, peace, happiness, privacy (etc.) are all good answers. However, it is a trick-question. We are not entitled to anything since a) everything requires our attention and b) it would be hypocritical to complain about someone else's sense of entitlement while ignoring our own.

Try having your students say silk three times. Silk. Silk. Silk. What does a cow drink? Most people say "milk." But cows don't drink milk. And have them say "roast" three times. Roast. Roast. Roast. What do you put in your toaster? Most people will say toast. No, it is bread that we put in the toaster. This can be used to illustrate that we have 60,000 thoughts a day, ninety-five percent of them are the same as yesterday and we are influenced by everything we see, hear, and encounter. We need to be mindful. It's as simple as that.

The IDC4O course is about teaching students to not only dream but to realize their dreams. When my principal came into my IDC4O class to observe me teach as part of my evaluation year that I must undergo as a teacher in Ontario once every five years, I did another wonderful meditation in the chapel that he especially liked and that the students liked but I also taught the students about actual dreams. You don't have to be a psychiatrist to know that dreams can mean things if we interpret them. If you are like me, you usually do not remember all of your dreams. In *The Hidden Power of Dreams* by Denise Linn, she says, "The single most important element in remembering dreams is motivation. To acquire that motivation, you must first perceive your dreams as worthwhile; regard them as valuable messages received from your subconscious. It's imperative that you believe they deserve to be heard." And she goes on to list powerful affirmations that promote the recalling of dreams.

I am proud to say that several months into this course, one of the students told me they purchased Louise Hay cards. She loves them. Now she, and many others like her, have begun keeping a gratitude- journal. I think every family should have affirmation cards and each person in the family pick a card a week, and support the other as they work on their weekly focus.

CHAPTER 25

BRINGING OUR SOULS TO THE CLASSROOM

If we understand that evolution is the progression of accumulated awareness, then perhaps, if we focus our collective awareness, we might just speed up the evolutionary process.

-Spontaneous Evolution-

There are no limits for us teachers if we use affirmations effectively. Affirmations in the home: Here are some general affirmations that I have used. It is best to write them down and say them at least once a day. It is ideal to write them in a journal or as I have mentioned, I use *The Secret Gratitude Book*. Some of these are taken or based directly on Louis Hay affirmations. I won't share all my affirmations with you since they are personal (health and relationship affirmations will tend to be the most custom-made). For some of these you may wish to put "I am in the process of..." in front of the affirmation if you do not yet believe the affirmation to be true.

-I release the past and am grateful that it has brought me new awareness

-I now chose to believe it is easy for me to make changes

-I feel good about myself and am therefore naturally attractive

-I am non-judging

-I am patient

-I eat less

-I am changing and growing through the challenges that come my way. Although imperfect, I strive for perfection by loving and being loved. I cloak myself in radiant light and love. I arm myself with peace and optimism. Only the best of myself is available to brighten the path of those who accompany me along the way. I am strong, healthy, and vibrant

-I am fit, I am healthy

-I have energy

-I am budgeting

-I am happy

-I am always on time

-I remember everything when packing

-I feel great

-I'm thankful for my family friends, job, co-workers

-I am confident

-My presence is felt when I enter a classroom

-I am falling in love with life and therefore, every limitation is vanishing and the barriers and limitations on money, energy, health, luck, and happiness are broken. I have no resistance and am filled with unlimited energy as I unleash the power within me

-I am tough

-I drive the speed limit

-My skin is healthy and attractive

-I'm debt free

-I exude confidence

-I sleep well

-I get enough water

-My brain is active, healthy, and always branching out

-I see with love and hear with compassion

-I am now willing to see only my gifts/talents

-I dispel laziness

-I exercise

-Change is good, change is safe

-I have no reason to despair and every reason to never give up

-I am aware of my breathing

-Loving and approving of myself creates organization

-I am prosperous

-I am eternally young

-I am filled with love and affection

-I am joyous/happy/free/healthy

-I'm grateful for..... (list several things here)

-Blessings upon my car

-I love my job

-I have stress-hardiness (This affirmation is based on the book *Full Catastrophic Living)*

-I have spiritual wisdom and insight

-I always have excess money

-I love seeing myself making healthy choices

-I am mindful of past abundances (list them here...)

-More and more, I learn about and live according to healthy habits so my body is always equipped to handle challenges.

-The inspiration in me relieves stress

-Each and every day, I am open and receptive to meeting new people whom I enjoy knowing and who enjoy knowing me

-I refute my ego's non-logical negative thoughts

-I create the time to do what matters

-I am mature enough to avoid gossip

-I am healthy today and therefore healthy tomorrow

-When I catch myself having a negative thought, I say "Ah-ha! Nice try pain-body! This is an old thought, I no longer choose to think that way" (this is an important but hard affirmation. It will take a long time before this affirmation becomes second- nature but better you use it and it work seventy-five percent of the time than not use it at all, likewise the affirmation: When there is a problem I say in repetition: "All is well. Everything is working out for my highest good. Only good will come out of this.")

-My job, though I love it, is merely a stepping stone to far greater positions

Remember affirmations don't have to be all words:

-You can write down *breath* *love* which for me means to take three deep breaths and only say the word "love" it is a mini-meditation or *breath* *virtuous action.*

When you are making report cards, you will come across opportunities to transform some of them into affirmations. If you go back and look at the Ontario Catholic Graduate Expectations, those would make good affirmations for your students of any age.

If you find that you have taken this seriously and have implemented affirmations and there is no real change after three months, take comfort in the knowledge that it took me more than three months. Also, I would refer you to the book *The Everything Law of Attraction Book* by Meera Lester, specifically, chapter 15: "Manifesting Success in Your Career" whereby you will find a method for charting a course for success. Lester states that there are many reasons why career affirmations fail: "...a conflict between your core values and those of the company... Perhaps you are expected to do something that conflicts with your ethics... Since your beliefs lead to your thoughts about things, consider that you may first need to examine your beliefs since many of them were taught to you as a child.... Start with your intent to fill a need, something like: "My purpose/desire/intent is to create/develop/foster/provide/nurture/build ______________________ ______________________________________.'" She goes on in great detail about manifesting a raise, promotion, or dream job.

You are now ready for some more classroom/school affirmations:

-I keep the energy in the room high while maintaining a positive learning environment at all times

-I encourage students to pay attention (that's an important one!)

You are wise to phrase some of your intentions in the third person:

-Robbie D encourages students to participate verbally

or

-You allow students to integrate new information by giving the answer out loud

You can phrase some of your intentions to apply to your whole staff:

-The teachers at my school:

- help students to remember what they've learned because they hear it out loud from the entire group

-set the tone for high-participation learning

-make students feel they are part of the learning process

-update their class website frequently (I suggest every three days)

Whenever you are at a professional development workshop, conference, or network, take notes and transform some of them into affirmations (this will also help you avoid falling asleep at the more boring ones!). Whenever you are reading professional development literature, have your affirmation journal with you and transform some of the teachings into affirmations. For example, Michael Losier talks about changing the energy in the room accordingly, see if you can imagine changing some or all of these into affirmations:

"Have the students stand up and stretch, encourage the students to applaud after someone gives an answer, change your own position on the podium or at the front of the room. Stand in one place when telling a story, then move to another place when asking a question. Change your position when you change the subject." Or when he talks about sharing in small groups effectively and what that does: "Students integrate the information as they share it with others, students will feel empowered as they share and learn with others in the group, hearing what others have to say heightens the learning experience for all, and the trainer or teacher will see and hear how well the students have engaged in and learned the information being taught."

No matter how well Teachers College is set up, there are moments of rude awakenings for teachers when they begin their career. Many teachers cry on their first day. Many, myself included, look back on their first year as their hardest year. And there is an exodus of teachers from the profession in the first five years. For many, there is a shock to the system when they realize how many students procrastinate. Students who procrastinate cause countless problems. But wait a minute, many teachers procrastinate too. I know the difference between my effectiveness at the front of the class when my day plan has the week lined out and I'm caught up on my marking versus when I'm teaching and I haven't the next day planned for and I'm three weeks behind in marking. It's impossible to expect your students to overcome procrastination when you yourself can't. However, it should be clear by now that affirmations can rid you quickly of that nasty addiction. Then what? There are many so-called strategies that I've heard plugged at many workshops by speakers who spend their time out of the class and going around talking to teachers and their strategies aren't practical. "Be patient with your students" is easier said then done. It can work for maybe one day. The students who annoy us the most are like so many other students we find in every school and yet ironically, these students think that their behavior is unique or charming and I've been in the staff room when teachers argue over whether or not a certain student is funny or not. When we talk about our students in the staff room we need to be careful not because the window might be open or a teacher might be on the phone, though often times teachers forget about that too, but because we are making strong affirmations when we talk about our students. Be careful if you are saying negative things that aren't helpful and don't make you or anyone feel better. Also, be careful if saying something positive that is only positive to you. If I am having major issues with a student and you tell me how much of an angel he or she is with you how do you think that will make me feel? I'm likely to infer that what you are really saying is, "I'm a better teacher than you, and if you are having problems with this student you must be doing something wrong." It is conceited to say "Oh I never have problems with Billy, Johnny, Sally, Ryan, or Cody or whomever, never." What good is there in that? It's all so silly. You could say, "Hmmm..... that doesn't sound like so-and- so, have you tried (name something that works for you)?

If you want I can talk to him/her for you." Some teachers go running to their principal or union rep when a fellow co-worker tells them about a student they are having problems with that the other teacher also teaches or coaches. I respect the teacher's right to want nothing to do with your behavior management because it's their own lack of virtuous action that will work against them not you. So again, what do we do? I don't know how many times I have been told that problem students are grieving something in their lives and there are deeper issues. I always want to say, "OK... so.... are you saying we should ignore the problem till it goes away?" Procrastination is a bad habit and bad habits can be broken. And that is a statement of fact you can tell your student in question because they already know they are a procrastinator. Tell them that when you are a procrastinator you develop a reputation as one and nobody wants that. The problem is procrastinators usually don't want to change because their habit is working for them. Try meeting with a student on your prep period taking them out of class for a minute or two to talk to them, they won't give you attitude here because they won't mind being pulled out of class as much as they do lunch. And now you can affirm that you have started a process and you will continue to try until there are wonderful results. We all know that praise works. Sometimes we can't bring ourselves to praise students and this is a negative affirmation. Students consistently get the same marks, maybe they always get a 52 (aka a D- or a 1-), but almost all students sooner or later get a mark above their average. I think this is when it is most important to jump all over that with praise. Affirmations can only help. We know that getting angry with them is a waste of time and the longer we have been teaching the more true we know this to be. I've never heard a teacher say, "I just get angry with them, that works."

Chances are that behavior problem students have an uncomfortable home-life and have a parent or several family members who get angry with them and anger does not work in the classroom for the same reason it does not work in the home. It causes animosity and resentment. It causes wounds. Students want attention. In this sense, we really do need to give them more of what they want and we need it to be more positive and less negative. When it's the other way around, we will be going home at the end of the day and getting up in the morning thinking about how many days there are left until summer vacation. Of course that's just an expression, and here's why, all teachers know exactly at any given time how much longer until Christmas Break, Spring Break, and July/August but the teacher who is at peace practicing affirmations in their class and life is ready to go back in September and is looking forward to it whereas the alternative is you going back in literal denial that the summer is over. If you have been teaching as long as I have you must be saying to yourself, "been there done that" since I have never met anyone that considered themselves a master teacher in their first year of teaching. Again, with any discipline, how we phrase our wording is as important as our tone. A lot of workshops on classroom management talk about this. Accusation phrases like "You started this mess" and "You never listen" are not effective. "You never..." and "You always..." are often disastrous. "You always misbehave" is said by many a teacher and of course if you were to put that on a report card comment, no principal would allow it. Negative rhetorical questions can get you into trouble like "Why are you being so selfish?" Imagine saying to a parent in an interview, "Your kid is so selfish." Just because a statement is true doesn't mean it is wise to say it. But our ego certainly sees it that way doesn't it? You would never, at least I hope never, say to a student "You're an idiot" or "What drugs are you on?" But many of us would or have used this type of language with our own friends, family, or co-workers. And most of us have had people likewise talk to us this way. And we know how it makes us feel. So imagine how it makes your students feel when they get all kinds of signals from you that you think they are delinquent or idiotic; in terms of affirmations, you might as well be name-calling. Some of us adults are insult- comics and have no problem saying to someone to "Fuck Off" and mean it in a purely joking way and if the other person is likewise a fellow insult- comic, they will respond with a smile and they won't take offense. If this is you, I hope you realize that strong negatively charged loaded- language can't be positive anymore than positive language can be negative. For the record, I am not an insult-comic. What is so humorous about insulting someone or embarrassing someone you consider a friend?

Read any of the research done by Dr. Emuto (eg. *The Healing Properties of Water*). In a nutshell, he had many samples of water and studied the water molecules under electron microscopes and documented the differences between water that was blessed, prayed over, meditated over, had words like "love" and 'peace" taped to their beakers versus the results of water samples with swear words and words like "hate", "666" (etc) on them. If our thoughts can do that to water, what can they do to our minds and bodies? Emuto has invaluable teachings about water and even shows that students learn better when they are hydrated and many of them now more than ever are not.

Many students get less than 1 (l) of water a day and humans need around 2(l) of water a day not to mention we need even more than the recommend daily intake when we are under stress. Teachers take note!

Mind effecting biology is something we don't consider enough. Many people dismiss it and yet it's obvious enough when someone is embarrassed and their face turns red or when a sad thought causes tears. We all know that stress can cause all kinds of problems. Now is the time for us to progress past this point in history.

Here is the most important paragraph in the whole book. We need to increase our understanding and conviction that we are composed of energy. Integrating this truth into our lives will empower people to live every day in the conscious understanding that every thought directly affects and shapes our world. Students could go out into the world secure in the knowledge that they can take the gifts of education and affirmations and build a life filled with success and joy. Therefore, what we need is authentic mindfulness which leads to internal coherence. Understanding this phenomenon in the classroom begins with understanding a few general examples of internal coherence. Consider this:

-if you swing a large pendulum and lots of smaller ones and then leave and come back later, they will be swinging in sync.

-if you hit a tuning fork, nearby tuning forks will vibrate at the same speed.

-the heart entrains other organs so when it is coherent and healthy so too our body.

So, in a classroom when the teacher brings their A-game, the students are much more likely to learn and put more effort into the class since the teacher is illustrating a maximum effort too. This explains why so many teachers teach their best lessons when they are being appraised and the principal is in the classroom. Considering this knowledge, teacher performance appraisal observations are not authentic evaluations. But there are three ways to interpret this fact and only one is healthy:

1. The anti-unionist will say: "The incompetent teacher knows

when s/he is being observed and will prepare a good lesson. The principal should pop in the class unannounced."

2. The anti-administration teacher will say: "The principal has no right to come in unannounced because s/he could come in on an off-day."

3. The mindful teacher will say: "the mindful principal will offer valuable constructive feedback to one and all, excellent and less than satisfactory teachers alike."

Like anything in education, all this depends on teachers buying into it. We don't know enough yet about the long-term benefits of mindfulness. Someday, teachers may be the clairvoyants of the world. When there is something that you know without knowing how you know it's called "claircognizance" or 'clear knowing.' If a teacher masters mindfulness they can know or at least understand well enough, why a student is behaving the way they are or performing the way they are. I'm not yet at this point but some teachers are aren't they? This is the ultimate in pro-activeness. Imagine it! I have experienced "claircognition". I have stated facts that I could not prove were facts and said when pressed, "that's what I think" and later it would be proven that it was a fact as I had suggested. Another example was when the magnitude-5 earthquake hit Ontario on June 23rd, 2010 (felt in Cleveland, Boston, Windsor, Toronto, Ottawa, and Montreal), I was in the staff room and none of us had experienced an earthquake before (there hadn't been one that moderate/severe since the 1940's) and I would never have thought that it was an earthquake, I thought that there were phys.ed students running on the second floor above us, but one of the teachers immediately said, "That was an earthquake boys." He was able to rule out other possibilities like an explosion. Intuition is not always right, claircognizance is. We can affirm that we look forward to enabling this ability we all have within us. Affirm: "Like great inventors, scientists, authors, futurists, and leaders all who had great teachers in their lives, I take the gifts of my education and apply it to the collective- unconscious and access new ideas and inspiration." I say "gifts of education" because as teachers we are capable of higher-learning and that is what is expected of us. It is what we should expect of ourselves. We should be avid readers and pursue professional development if we are to tap into intellectual awareness in real terms. Affirm: "I am thinking-orientated." I remember teaching students about the 1000 Monkeys theory that says there is no such thing as original thought in that any idea or concept that is thought of or any invention or innovation that is conjured up in a mind will likewise be conjured up in other minds as well. If Alexander Graham Bell had not invented the phone someone else would have. The name comes from a group of moneys that were oddly washing their fruit before they ate it and then a separate group of monkeys on a remote island nowhere near the other monkeys and having no way of having contact with those monkeys was observed doing the same thing. Let us be aware of infinite possibilities. Affirm: "New helpful knowledge comes effortlessly to me often." Wouldn't you like to see that on your report card comment: "Johnny generally deciphers new helpful knowledge without assistance."

I heard a superintendent in my board once say, "The long goodbye begins long before high school." My hope is that mindfulness in education begins in the primary grades and continues on to grade twelve. And even if we have students who come to high school with all kinds of behavior issues, I am reminded by something that same superintendent said, "It's never too late to intervene."

The last time I received my Summative Report Form for Experienced Teachers as part of my Teacher Performance Appraisal, I thought it was a great opportunity for me to feel gratitude for the improvements I had made since my previous one, but also to convert a lot of the wording into affirmations such as the following (if you give some of these a try as affirmations, you can't go wrong):

I adapt and refine my teaching practices through continuous learning and reflection, using a variety of sources and resources

I use appropriate technology in my teaching and related professional responsibilities

I consistently deliver the appropriate curriculum

I teach the curriculum by exhibiting an understanding and ability to explain subject areas

I can discuss subject matter from provincial and board documents with my students with confidence

I consistently demonstrate knowledge of and am able to follow and explain appropriate legislation, local policies and procedures

I demonstrate a positive, professional attitude when communicating with parents and students

I employ the use of an outstanding classroom web page to ensure parents are informed of their child's progress

I communicate regularly with members of the English and Social Sciences departments (you would substitute here your appropriate departments)

I use ongoing reporting to keep both students and parents informed

I employ a variety of appropriate techniques to report student progress to my parent community

I demonstrate knowledge of trends, techniques and research relevant to my teaching

I assess and review program delivery for relevancy

I use provincial achievement standards and competency statements as a reference point for evaluation of teaching

I reflect on teaching effectiveness that is shaped by human development and learning

I integrate curriculum expectations effectively into teaching practice

I effectively modify programs effectively to respond to the needs of exceptional students

I always seek guidance from the school administration on areas that I need clarification and consultation

I use a variety of effective resources to enhance the learning of my students

I use a variety of appropriate teaching techniques to engage my students

I systemize routine procedures and tasks to engage students in varied learning experiences

In my class, students are provided with opportunities to share their interests and demonstrate their involvement in learning

I modify my programs to fit students' needs by making topics relevant to students' lives and experiences

I adapt and select themes according to my students' abilities which greatly assists me in providing a nurturing learning environment

I demonstrate care and respect for students by maintaining positive interactions

I employ effective questioning techniques that encourage higher level thinking skills for my students

And now, some general closing affirmations:

I am proud to be a teacher

I am a great teacher and I get better and better each and every day

Teaching is one of the most honorable and noble of all professions

I love what I do and know that my enthusiasm is contagious

I bring knowledge, dedication, and understanding to my classroom

My students will be better people because of me, and I will be a better person because of them

I know what I give to my students will come back to me in many wonderful and unexpected ways

I am an awesome teacher

I realize that everything has a highest potential including a way to teach and a way to answer a question

I realize that advise comes from the ego and counsel comes from the soul

My students have my absolute commitment

I give my students all I can so that tomorrow they can be all they can

Each and every day, I bring knowledge and dedication to my classroom

I love teaching! At the end of every day, I KNOW I have made a difference

I am a great teacher! I am a great teacher! I am a great teacher and I get better and better each and every day

I am a great teacher! Each day I strive to be that teacher my students will look back on an say, "Thanks!"

I thrive on making [fill in your subject] relevant to the lives of my students and today I do

A great teacher lives within me! Today that teacher is shaping futures

I stay focused by remembering why I got into teaching

Each and every day, I share life's greatest gift – the gift of learning

I am a happy person because I register the positive over the negative; this Velcro versus Teflon approach to perspective only takes twenty seconds

I realize the power of positive praise

Just like the bright summer sun, I am a radiant being in my classroom; My students feel safe and warm in my presence

If you walk away from this book learning only one thing... I hope it is that if you want the perfect classroom, then give love by imagining and feeling yourself with the classroom you love, instead of imagining and feeling that you have the class from Hell every single day. If you haven't even gotten that much out of it because you believe that it's a bunch of hoopla, simply put it to the beyond chance test and affirm that you are attracting something unusual into your life. Imagine it, feel it, and prepare to receive it. Then you should be more convinced that the law of attraction works. Examples include choosing to attract a specific flower or receiving an unexpected letter in the mail.

"Hugging myself and saying "I love you" is something very powerful in my life. I just hold myself, like a loving parent cradling a precious child, and I feel safe. Most important, I feel loved. I still have bad days, but now when I have them, I simply remind myself that this is one of those times when I need to love myself more instead of going into a spiral of depression." - Marcela, What One Good Hug Can Do (Modern-Day Miracles)

FLOW WITH IT, AN AFTERWORD

"I am in the process of positive change. I am unfolding in fulfilling ways. Only good can come to me. I now express health, happiness, prosperity, and peace of mind."

- Louise L. Hay-

Thank you for reading this book. I wish you clear horizons and wellness on your journey. And now some general things to note about affirmations and mindfulness and recommended readings:

You know, being a mindful-teacher and being a mindful-parent go hand in hand if you are a parent. Just imagine how amazingly easy our jobs would be if our students' parents were all mindful. Since most teachers are, or will be, parents, I recommend Laura-May Culver, who helps spread the word about mindful-parenting. Let's all be present with our children today and every day-- the children in our families, the children on our earth just as we are for our students. We can ALL be mindful parents and teachers and take care of each other.

For those of you who are not teachers or who are sharing the philosophy of this book with your non-teacher spouse, friends or family, I suggest, in terms of general workplace mindfulness 101, the book *The Power* where it states: "When you think about your job, your feelings tell you what you are giving about your job. If you feel good about your job, you must receive back positive circumstances and experiences in your job- because that is the positive feeling you're giving."

Some of you are fortunate enough to never have had terrible financial problems and experiences like I have. But my past can help illustrate that the law of attraction works. For years, I had bad credit, was in debt, and I hated bills and constantly complained that gas, cable, internet, food, houses, cars, and hydroelectricity were all over-priced. *The Power* states: "Never pay your bills when you don't feel good." In hindsight, I most certainly paid bills when I did not feel positive during those years and sometimes didn't pay them at all! There is also a difference between knowing that teachers are underpaid versus complaining that we don't get paid enough. I have encountered a select few in the profession who believe we are very well paid. I don't necessarily agree with this but I suspect that they are either married to someone who is well-off or have or will be inheriting a substantial amount of money or they simply are very positive thinkers. It's better to say you do get paid well enough and I know teachers who often say "we have it pretty good all around." That is a great attitude. *The Power* says: "When you receive your salary, be grateful for it so it multiplies!" Many times during my career I said, "I'm broke!" Or I would say on the Wednesday night before a pay-day, "I made it." And many times I can recall thinking on such a day that all of the money was spoken for by bills and I would not be looking forward to the next two weeks as a result. It's no wonder at all why I was living pay-cheque to pay-cheque. Now I have learned to be mindful of my money. *The Power* states: "Feel love when you hand over money!" It's time that creative people get creative with how they handle money to attract more money into their lives. For example, in *The Power* it is suggested: "Each time you handle money, deliberately flip the bills so the front is facing you." I don't know if this will attract lottery winnings and I would not advise it as an excuse to go to the casino, however, I for one have started doing it and I have a refreshed and energized attitude about the money I spend and earn.

I should point out that I remember the first time I read *The Power*, I didn't like the author saying: "I didn't give money away to bring more money to me. I gave it away so I would feel love about money." I thought, C'mon! What's the difference? She is telling us this story because it's HOW SHE GOT RICH! She's telling us that if we want more money we have to love money. I don't get it?! However, she was not always rich. Here's the way I see it now; send love to everything we do and as much as we can, including money. Feel love about money. Love money as an energy and a form of exchange. It's a quality of feeling attached to the wealth (love-based wealth rather than fear-based wealth). I also recall being confused by the author stating, "In business... you simply can't take from anyone" (i.e., you get what you give) and "You can't give love for money and then walk around being rude and negative to people, because if you do that, you open the door for negativity to walk into your finances." Well, I read that and originally thought what about big bad business like some of the oil cartels or some of the pharmaceuticals? Their lack of respect for us doesn't cut into their billions, does it? However, the old paradigm of unethical big business practices is falling apart --- it won't be long before it completely shifts. A new economy is emerging and there will be a turbulent period preceding it. Eventually, karma will catch up with heartless business owners. They cannot escape karma, they simply can't. It may seem to us like they've escaped it, but what seems like too many years to us is the blink of an eye from the quantum perspective. If they don't pay/learn the lesson of love in this life, they will most surely pay the next one. Look at companies like Enron and the like. Eventually, they do fall apart at the seams. It is not uncommon for a giant like Conrad Black to fall into demise seemingly overnight. It happens fast. Oh, and pharmaceuticals are starting to show losses as the paradigm of health-consciousness shifts. I was reading about how the Gardisal vaccination is a huge money loser and a disaster that was not expected to hit BigPharma. Furthermore, I recall taking issue to the author writing, "...if you stick a label on any person... you are sticking the label on you, and that's what you will receive." So I thought, does this mean I just have to suck it up when it comes to the computers at my school that don't work and haven't for years and the board very selfishly refuses to fix them? I realize now that I have to send love to the computers I have when so many in the world don't. I have to send love to all the computers that DO work (even if they are only found in the office) and all those that work outside the school like my trusty laptop. I have to send love to all the things computers HAVE DONE for my life to date. And I have to send love and be kind to my administrators as I do my job in a kind and conscientious way which may sometimes include respectfully pointing out the need for improvement. What they do with my kind request and advocacy work is their karma, not mine. Lastly, I was not impressed the first time I read the author say that nothing good ever comes out of arguing. BUT, I thought, what about defending yourself leading in turn to an apology given by the other person, no? I still don't have any problems with respectful arguing; as long as the arguing comes from a place of love and compassion for self and others. The need to defend is fear-based protection of ego, not compassion-based protection of a loving relationship. For more on this, read Thich Nhat Hanh or Pema Chodron.

What I would suggest is the following: Live your life TOTALLY based on the *Power* rules. Don't cheat. Do this for three months. Be serious and be willing to put your reservations and disbelief on hold for only three months. Document everything that you notice and then decide if it's worth trying for another three to six months. Ask for signs from your spirit guides to let you know if you're on the right track.

I hope with all sincerity you have found some useful teacher affirmations that you can use but remember that you must always remember to use general life affirmations outside the school setting as well. Try filling in the following blanks to make some that apply to you personally:

> ______________________________ is improving every day
>
> It feels good to ______________________________
>
> I have decided to ______________________________
>
> I am always ______________________________
>
> ______________________________ is what I want to do and
>
> ______________________________ is what I can do
>
> I use my inner resources and beliefs to maximize my
>
> ______________________________
>
> *(energy, memory, clarity, calmness, joy, peace, being present, awareness, inner strength, courage, empowerment, organization, self-confidence, self-worth, self-love, support, ability to see bigger picture....)*

Take gentle care of yourself. Be well. Remember, the way you chose to think right now is just that, a choice. It's like The Tragically Hip say, "it's a good life if you don't have to weakin'." Think well of your administrators, talk to your supply-teachers and make them feel welcomed as opposed to invisible and wish wellness right now to your co-workers, parents, and students. Above all, and always, enjoy your family and your peace.

> "I choose to be strong by being soft and pliable rather than inflexible, brittle, and hard."
>
> - Dr. Wayne Dyer-

Further recommended reading (In addition to the sources I have referred to and/or quoted in this book, please also consider some or all of the following valuable resources):

1. www.abraham-hicks.com ("The most magnificent Creators don't want to get together with people who think just like they do. They're looking for people who have other thoughts, because out of the contradiction, comes ideas that could not be born out of sameness. Your relationships will be ultimately more if you're not identical twins just "yessing, yessing, yessing" to everything that the other one is about.") --- Abraham-- Excerpted from the workshop in Los Angeles, CA on Saturday, July 24th, 1999

2. Meetup.com (find fun support groups) (eg. in my area, http://www.meetup.com/Law-of-Attraction-Ottawa/)

3. An Apple a Day: 'Teachers, Be of Good Courage' (Inspiring thoughts for teachers at the start of the new school year. BY: Vicki Caruana): http://www.beliefnet.com/Inspiration/Christian-Inspiration/2003/09/An-Apple-A-Day-Teachers-Be-Of-Good-Courage.aspx

4. *13 Teacher Affirmations – The Affirmation Spot for Tuesday March 16, 2010* Ray Davis http://theaffirmationspot.wordpress.com/2010/03/16/13-teacher-affirmations/

5. Positive affirmations for students: http://searchwarp.com/swa21801.htm

6. Healyourlife.com

7. hayhouseradio.com

8. Louise Hay YouTube channel

9. Louise Hay on Facebook and Twitter

10. greggbraden.com

11. brianweiss.com

12. happyfornoreason.com

13. *Mindful Teaching And Teaching Mindfulness- A Guide For Anyone Who Teaches Anything.* By: Deborah Schoeberelin with Suki Sheth, PH.D. (a must-read for teachers! This book talks about being in the moment to infuse the classroom with openness, presence, and caring and goes more in detail in terms of breathing and journaling. "Teaching mindfulness directly to students augments the effects of the teacher's presence by coaching youth to exercise simple, practical, and universal attention skills themselves." She shows how there is a noticeable difference in students' performance when they learn mindfully versus when they do tasks mindlessly; "When students are *really there,* the classroom is alive with learning and their work shines." It is no wonder that my ENG3C and my CH2P students were chaotic since they were often disengaged or distracted. When we leave work for a supply/substitute-teacher, we often leave busy seat-work and we may think it saves us and the other teacher work. She talks about mindful eating which I think is important for teachers as we often rush through our lunch in the staffroom. She does a good job illustrating the importance of mindfulness in that little window between the time we get to school and the time our students arrive. Also, what we should do at the end of the day via purposeful action and intentions for tomorrow and general reflections (I know I have made the mistake of developing the routine of rushing out of school as soon as the buses are gone which is wrong on many levels). I love this book because it is practical and very realistic insomuch as it does not imply that mindfulness will make you invulnerable: "Mindfulness won't take you anywhere other than here. Living mindfully won't transform you into someone new- you'll simply experience and express your "you-ness" more directly with more creative energy. The same old routines can still structure your day. However, it is more likely that cultivating mindfulness will bring freshness to the experience of familiar events.").

14. *Psychic Protection- Creating Positive Energies for People and*

Places. By: William Bloom. This book is helpful for teachers. It is based on the concept that energy never disappears. We can shed light on why things go wrong in the classroom when they do, for example, "When someone has a tantrum, the energy and atmosphere of the tantrum may float way beyond the person actually having it and be felt by someone a great distance away." Other key quotes: "The body language of calm awareness is the same body language of the most accomplished confident fighter." "If you are panicking, there is no psychological space to work out what to do." Bloom talks about the perils of procrastination, why we do it, and what we can do about it. Also, he talks about the perils of exhaustion (it is here where we are "psychically vulnerable."). He teaches the easy strategies for staying centered and empowered in difficult situations or unpleasant atmospheres, and what you can do to change them.

15. *Fractal Time.* By: Gregg Braden. Braden talks about how cycles are based on natural rhythms, "we can use the universal codes that govern everything from the movement of quantum particles to the shape of our galaxy in a formula that takes the guesswork out of finding the places in time we're searching for." I am convinced, based on Braden's work, that there are natural cycles in the education system as well. He does not state that specifically but gives other examples such as where he says, "… global economies and the stock market are indicators of the investor community's optimism or pessimism."

16. Anything by Louise Hay, Greg Briden, Marie Jones, Malcolm Gladwell, Mitch Albom, Bruce Lipton, and Deepak Chopera who I have quoted in this book and every time I read or listen to one of his works I learn something new. He is gifted at phrasing things that are scientific yet in laymen terms yet interesting. He coins new terms that will someday be seen in our curriculums such as "karmic debt" (no debt goes unpaid according to the law of attraction). Any and all of his work teach us that the heart is holistic and always knows the right answer. It has a computing ability far more accurate than anything within the limit of rational thought. There is spontaneous right decision

(infinite choice but there can only be one that is the right choice that benefits you and those around you).

17. *What the Bleep Do We Know- Discovering The Endless Possibilities For Altering Your Everyday Reality* by Willam Arntz, Betsy Chasse and mark Vicente. If you have seen the documentary of the same name, read this book anyway, it is different than the film. It is one of my favorites. "The difference between me at five and me now is that at five I didn't have much invested emotionally in the Universe being a certain way. Being "wrong" never was a concern. It was all learning. Now I keep reminding myself: In science there is no such thing as a failed experiment. Learning that what I was testing simply does not work is actually a success." I realize that it is important for us to get our students to ask more and more questions and not worry about failure since this book makes it clear that this leads to opening up new ways of being in the world via transformation, growing, outgrowing, and moving on.

18. *Zapped-Why Your Cell Phone Shouldn't Be Your Alarm Clock and 1,268 Ways to Outsmart the Hazards of Electronic Pollution* by: Ann Louise Gittleman. This is a crucial book to read and it is extremely relevant because it talks about mindful eating and dieting in ways that counter-act the side effects of the radiation and dirty electricity we are exposed to and that our students are bombarded with (cell phones, power distribution lines, cordless phones, dimmer switches, wi-fi, refrigerators, tools, TVs, fluorescent lighting, microwave ovens, electric razors (etc)). It also explains why some teachers and students feel tired all the time in cases where they are over-exposed to electromagnetic signals.

19. *How We Decide* By Jonah Lehrer. I did briefly mention this book but trust me, you'll want to read this book as you will have a deeper appreciation for why our students, and people in general, make dumb choices. For example it uses brain research to help explain "why we get cranky when we're hungry and tired: the brain is less able to suppress the negative emotions sparked

by small annoyances. A bad mood is really just a rundown prefrontal cortex."

20. *13 Steps to Teacher Empowerment- Taking a More Active Role in Your Community* By: Steven Zemelman and Harry Ross.

21. *What Really Matters in Response to Intervention- Research-Based Interventions.* By: Richard L. Allington (clear recommendations to guide classroom teachers in designing response to intervention programs).

22. *Clock Waters- Six Steps to Motivating and Engaging Disengaged Students Across Content Areas.* By: Stevi Quate and John McDermott.

23. *Full Catastrophe Living- Using the Wisdom of Your Body and Mind to face stress, Pain, and Illness* by Jon Kabat-Zinn, Ph.D. This is the most scientific book out there on mindfulness. Phys-ed teachers especially will like this as the focus in physical health. The book is written by a doctor who has carefully researched and studied instances where tumors and other serious illnesses have been known to regress or disappear altogether without medical treatment. There is one key quote that helps explain why many of our dysfunctional students are struggling in all areas: "...loneliness, separation, and divorce are sometimes associated with reduced immune functions and the practice of relaxation techniques can have enhancing effects.

24. *The Field- The Quest for the Secret Force of the Universe* by: Lynne McTaggart. This book adds science to what our spiritual leaders have been saying long before the invention of the microscope: "...we and all the matter of the universe are literally connected to the furthest reaches of the cosmos through the Zero Point Field waves of the grandest dimensions...Everything in your world, anything you can hold in your hand, no matter how dense, how heavy, how large, on its most fundamental level boils down to a collection of electric charges interacting with a background sea of electromagnetic and other energetic fields- a kind of electromagnetic drag force."

25. *The Mindful Brain- Reflection and Attunement in the Cultivation of well-Being* by: Daniel J. Siegel: "...as we find a way to attune to our minds, an emerging sense of freedom and inner security becomes available in our lives."

26. *The Follow- Through Factor- Getting from Doubt to Done* by: Gene C. Hayden: "...the very act of smiling, regardless of how you actually feel, causes brain activity that is typically associated with good feelings... puff out your chest and strut, and you'll start to actually feel more confident."

27. *The Power of Your Subconscious Mind- There Are no Limits to the Prosperity, Happiness, and Peace of Mind You can Achieve Simply by Using the Power of the Subconscious Mind* by: Joseph Murphy, Ph.D. D.D. This book does a great job pin-pointing how to deal with difficult people: "...the temptation is to turn their negative energy back on them in the form of dislike. But to do that, you have to first take their negative energy into yourself, with all the bad effects that will have on your own being." If our thoughts transmit compassion and understanding we will be just fine, in fact it will "set in motion the process of changing them" (the difficult person/pupil/people).

28. *Quantum Shift in the Global Brain- How the New Scientific Reality can Change Us and Our World* by: Ervin Laszlo. This book has a chapter on the akashic field. It also has advice for teachers: "Encourage young people and open-minded people of all ages to evolve the spirit that could empower them to make ethical decisions of their own on issues that decide their future and the future of their children."

29. *Meditation for Beginners* by: Jack Kornfield. This was the first book and CD I ever used for class meditations when I first taught World Religions. It's an excellent starting point. The focus here is restorative justice: "Forgiveness is one of the key arts of the spiritual life because when we forgive others, we are able to release the past and start life anew. Without forgiveness, we are always left with 'who did what to whom,' repeating the cycle over and over."

30. *Teaching Teenagers- Making connections in the Transition Years* by: Jean D. Hewitt. I saw Jean Hewitt at my board when I was in my first year of teaching. I was amazed at her expertise. Her work has helped me in many ways. There are teacher checklists that make for good affirmations, for example:

"I praise high and low achieving students about the same amount when they are successful.

When I mark work, I try to give detailed and thoughtful feedback to all students whatever their abilities.

I have a positive, success-orientated classroom atmosphere.

I give clear written and oral instructions for all assignments.

I attempt to be conversational and friendly to all my students.

I expect the best they can give from each of my students, I don't settle for less."

31. *Playing Fair: A Guide to the Management of Student Conduct* by: Jean D. Hewitt.

32. *Positive Energy- 10 Extraordinary Prescriptions for Transforming Fatigue, Stress & Fear Into Vibrance, Strenght & Love* by: Judith Orloff, M.D. This handy book has a reference guide to energy exercises. As you know, I love it when authors keep it real too. She says prayer can lead to miracles but also points out: "Just because your dreams aren't manifesting now doesn't mean they never will. There's an integrity to how our lives flow."

33. *Stillness Speaks* by: Eckhart Tolle. This book teaches you how to break unconscious identification with negative thoughts: "Little stories we tell ourselves, often in the form of complaints (are) unconsciously designed to enhance our always deficient sense of self... (creating) some kind of enemy: yes, the ego needs enemies to define its boundry, and even the weather can serve that function." Hmmm.... I really was over-reacting when

I complained to the hotel that their pool wasn't heated when I went to Florida on Christmas Break and it was freezing outside the whole time… I now invest in affirmation-based vacations.

34. *You can Heal Your Life Companion Book* by Louise Hay. I have read all her books and highly recommend each and every one of them. I have so much trust in Louise Hay and am thankful that she released this text book whereby each section is based on a different aspect of life such as relationships, health, or workplace (etc.). The section most beneficial to teachers and/or students would be that of "critical thinking." You are walked through a series of reflection questions and mirror-work and end up with affirmations like "I release the need to criticize others."

35. *101 Exercises for the Soul- A Divine Workout Plan for Body, Mind, and Spirit* by: Dr. Bernie S. Siegel

36. *365 Energy Boosters* by Susannah Seton and Sondra Kornblatt.

37. *The Four Agreements- Toltec Wisdom Collection* by: Don Miguel Ruiz.

38. *The Law of Attraction* by Deanna Davis, PhD.

39. Louise L. Hay & Friends- *The Times of Our Lives- Extraordinary True Stories of Synchronicity, Destiny, Meaning, and Purpose* compiled & edited by: Jill Kramer

40. *The Everything Law of Attraction Book- Harness the power of Positive Thinking and Transform Your Life* by: Meera Lester

41. *The Doctors Book of Home Remedies* by: the editors of "Prevention" Magazine Health Books.

42. *Training the Mind- and Cultivating Loving-Kindness* by: Chogyam Trungpa.

43. *Ten Poems to Change Your Life* by: Roger Housden

44. *2013* by Marie Jones

45. *The Law of Attraction* and *The Astonishing Power of Emotions* by: Esther and Jerry Kicks (The Teachings of Abraham).

46. *Addicted to Unhappiness* by: Martha Heineman Pieper, PH.D. and William J. Pieper, M.D.

47. *Good Morning- 365 Positive Ways to start Your Day* by: Brook Noel.

48. *Affirmations* by: Stuart Wilde.

49. *Soul Wisdom* by: Dr. Zhi Gang Sha

50. *One Day My Soul Just Opened Up* by: Iyanla Vanzant.

www.ingramcontent.com/pod-product-compliance
Lightning Source LLC
Chambersburg PA
CBHW022017090426
42739CB00006BA/170
* 9 7 8 1 4 5 2 5 3 2 6 2 2 *